DON'T GO TO
UNCLE'S
WEDDING

CW00952061

DON'T GO TO UNCLE'S WEDDING

Voices from the Warsaw Ghetto

JENNY ROBERTSON

Published in Great Britain in 2000 by
Azure
1 Marylebone Road
London
NW1 4DU

British Library Cataloguing-in-Publication Data

A catalogue record for this book is available from the
British Library

ISBN 1–902694–11–2

Typeset by Pioneer Associates, Perthshire
Printed in Great Britain by
Caledonian International Ltd, Glasgow

Contents

Acknowledgements

My first thanks are to the memoir writers whose voices prompted this book – and to those who edited their diaries, postcards and letters. My warm thanks also go to Ms Miroslawa Bobrowska in the bookshop of the Jewish Historical Institute for her unfailing help. I also want to thank Regina Żagan for her friendship and support. Jonathan Luxmoore gave me the benefit of his experience and kindly looked at the manuscript. Barbara Schwitz and Eileen Elliot, together with other members of the Warsaw Writers' Group, offered useful criticism. Brigitte is a fellow-traveller who offered her support in Poland and across the miles. I want to thank Naomi Starkey of the Bible Reading Fellowship for encouraging me not to give up in the early stages and Alison Barr of Azure for her help and editing.

But my biggest debt, day in day out, has been to my husband Stuart, who patiently shared his knowledge of language, not least of Polish, and his encyclopaedic mind. He also cooked meals, hunted down addresses, brought me coffee, iced drinks, insight, humour and in every sense was my companion through the Warsaw ghetto.

Polish Names

Polish consonants look formidable, but they never break rules! *Sz*, for example, sounds like English 'sh'; *cz* sounds like English 'ch'. With this in mind the name of Dr Janusz Korczak, whom we shall meet in the book, presents no problem: it sounds like Janush Korchak. Similarly Anielewicz sounds like An–yel–ev–ich. The letters *ch*, however, sound like 'ch' in Scots.

Szcz looks impossible, but say 'English cheese' – and you have it exactly. The Jewish Fighting Force was known as ŻOB. The first letter sounds exactly like the sound the French have in the word for 'I' : *je*. So say ŻOB as if you were practising for *'Allo, 'Allo* – and you will have 'j'ob'. Polish *u* sounds like 'oo' in English, and so does Polish *ó*. So the city of Kraków sounds like Krakoov. Polish also has a second 'l' – it is written with a line through it and sounds like English 'w'. Put these sounds together and the city of Łódź, which we shall meet in the book, sounds exactly like Woodge.

Sources and Acknowledgements

The author and publisher acknowledge with thanks permission to use material from the following publications. The titles in the left-hand column are the abbreviations used in this book.

Accuse   Maria Hochberg-Mariańska, Noe Gruss (eds)
       Jewish Children Accuse (Dzieci Żydowskie
       Oskarżają), Shalom Foundation, Warsaw,
       1993.

Children   Wiktoria Śliwowska (ed.) *Holocaust Children*
       Speak, Society of Children of the Holocaust
       in Poland, Warsaw, 1993. English translation,
       The Last Eyewitnesses, Children of the Holocaust
       Speak, Northwestern University Press,
       Evanston, Illinois, 1999.

Chronicle   Emanuel Ringelblum, *Chronicle of the Warsaw*
       Ghetto (Kronika z getta warszawskiego),
       Czytelnik, Warsaw, 1988.

Diary   Adam Czerniaków, *Diary of the Warsaw Ghetto*
       (Dziennik z getta warszawskiego), ed. Martin
       Fuchs (German version translated by Silbke
       Lent, C. H. Beck, München, 1988).

Extermination
and Uprising Cywia Lubetkin, *Extermination and Uprising*
       (Zagłada i Powstanie), Jewish Historical
       Institute, Warsaw, 1999.

The Ghetto is Fighting	Marek Edelman, *The Ghetto is Fighting* (*Getto walczy*), Interpress, Warsaw, 1988.
Homeland	Władysław Bartoszewski and Zofia Lewinówna (eds), *This Person is from my Homeland* (*Ten jest z ojczyzny mojej*), Znak, Kraków, 1969.
Letters	Ruta Sakowska (ed.), *Letters about Extermination* (*Listy o Zagładzie*), PWN, Warsaw, 1997.
Memoirs	Michał Grynberg (ed.), *Memoirs from the Warsaw Ghetto* (*Pamiętniki z getta warszaw-skiego*), PWN, Warsaw, 1988. An English translation is in preparation as *The Warsaw Ghetto Diaries*, Metropolitan Books, Henry, Holt and Company Inc., USA.
Remnants	Jan Jagielski, Tomasz Lec, *Remnants of the Warsaw Ghetto* (*Ślady z getta warszawskiego*), Jewish Historical Institute, Warsaw, 1997.
Survive!	Tomasz Grosse (ed.), *Survive!* (*Przeżyć!*), Trio, Warsaw, 1998.
Text	Jan Leociak, *Tekst wobec Zagłady* (*Text in the Face of Extermination*), Monografie FNP, Wrocław, 1997.

Prologue
'May this treasure fall into good hands . . .'

The subject of the Holocaust is so vast that we can never come to the end of it. We think we know – and then discover how little we know. This book focuses on one aspect of it: the story of the Warsaw ghetto.

I moved to Warsaw recently. One bright April morning not long after my arrival I felt swamped by sorrow. I went on to the balcony. A large group of young people had come crowding into the yard below. Later I caught up with them and they explained that they were visiting sites in Warsaw connected with the Holocaust – and that part of the ghetto wall was actually in my yard.

'We are now imprisoned behind a double wall: a wall of bricks for our bodies and a wall of silence for our souls. Everything that is done here, everything that happens is sealed off by total silence,' wrote Chaim Kaplan from within the Warsaw ghetto.[1]

People were sealed off, but red bricks remain as silent witnesses. A plaque fixed to the wall states: 'Between 1940 and 1941 this wall was the boundary of the ghetto'. Lower down the wall is a gap where bricks have been prised out and taken to the Holocaust Museum in Washington.

Across the yard is an unmarked piece of the wall and beyond, in the neighbouring courtyard, another part rises forbiddingly to its original height. There is a small memorial garden here, and a map of the ghetto. Two bricks have been removed from this section too and are now in Yad Vashem, the Holocaust museum in Jerusalem.

There's a school on the other side of the wall. Kids cluster in the yard to smoke illicit cigarettes. Smart young people come in Fiat cars to study Business English in the evenings. Cars race along the six-lane highway beyond. Skyscrapers soar to the heavens – these ambitious towers of business and tourism dwarf Stalin's unwanted gift to Poland: the Palace of Culture and Sciences, now almost hidden from view. And the fragments of the ghetto wall are now a focal point for tourists to Poland's capital city, which before the Second World War had boasted the second largest Jewish community in the world.

Silence hung over the murder of the Jews of Poland – and this silence lasted many years. I spent a year in Warsaw in 1964. I found only one sign which pointed to the Jewish life, wiped out 19 years before. This was the now world-famous monument to the heroes of the Warsaw ghetto. The majestic sculpture became a signpost for me – and the dreary Warsaw winter became haunted by presences less tangible than November mist or January sleet, but none the less real, although I am not a fanciful person, nor do I believe in ghosts.

Many people put their experiences into words. Enclosed within walls, hiding in cellars, even in the rubble between burning buildings, they wrote their stories. 'My writing is very untidy now because I can only write when I have light as I'm living mainly in the darkness of a cellar,' wrote one woman. Another diarist recorded: 'Someone's knocking, I stop writing so that they won't hear the scratching of my nib . . . It's dark now, I can't write any more because I mustn't strike a light.'[2]

Some were professional people who had kept diaries before the war and continued to do so now; others were driven by an inner force. Words burned within them and they couldn't keep silent. They wrote out of the extremities of their experience, literally on the border between life and death. Fathers whose children had been snatched away poured out their anguish in words, husbands tried to create memorials for their murdered wives with thin ink and coarse paper. Children wrote – one little girl thrust a note into the hands of the guard who was hustling her towards the train.

Some people managed to get letters through to relatives in Warsaw, even to toss a note from the train which was carrying them away for ever: 'We're going away tomorrow into the unknown . . .', 'We're going away to work . . . I can't give you our new address because we don't know it yet.'³

They wrote so that generations to come would hear their story, so that future tribunals of justice would speak on their behalf. They wrote, crying out for revenge, wrestling with the darkness.

In the Warsaw ghetto, memoirs and letters were collected by a secret group. They met on Saturdays, hence their name: *Oneg Shabat*, Sabbath Joy, Sabbath meeting. The guiding light was a historian, Dr Emanuel Ringelblum, who understood that what was happening was unprecedented in the history of the Jewish nation and it was therefore imperative that an accurate record should be kept. As early as October 1939, a month after the Germans occupied Poland and a year before the ghetto walls were built, Ringelblum laid the foundations for the Oneg Shabat Archives.

Only the barest handful of his colleagues survived, but in 1943, just before the Ghetto Uprising, these documents were hidden in milk churns and metal boxes beneath 68 Nowolipki

Street, the location of a secret school and a centre of the underground movement in the ghetto. And then in September 1946, in the ocean of rubble which was Warsaw, a survivor, Hersz Wasser, secretary of Oneg Shabat, picked his way across the ruins. Others were with him. At first they found nothing – but then their spades struck metal, and they brought up boxes and two sealed milk churns which held the stories of the Jews in Warsaw. A third container has never been found. The texts, in Yiddish, in Hebrew, in Polish, are kept within the archives of the Jewish Historical Institute in Warsaw. They have survived death and destruction, fire and flood. The members of Oneg Shabat buried these stories in the hope that they would 'fall into good hands', as one young man who participated in the sealing and concealing of the papers wrote. 'We have buried in the earth those things we couldn't shout out to the world. May this treasure fall into good hands, may it await better times, may it raise the alarm to the world which has gone astray in the twentieth century.'[4]

Those silenced voices draw us into the Warsaw ghetto where we confront a 'world which has gone astray . . .'

Notes

1 Quoted by Jan Leociak in *Text*.
2 *Text*.
3 *Letters*.
4 Quoted in Artur Eisenbach's introduction to *Chronicle*.

CHAPTER 1

Walled in

On 31 August 1939 the Gestapo staged an attack on a radio station in Gliwice, a town on the Polish border – and Hitler shocked the world by declaring himself obliged to commence hostilities. France and the United Kingdom entered the war on 3 September – but pre-war leaders had not taken accurate stock of the situation and Poland was left to fight alone.

'O, war, little darling, what a lady you are! All the painted boys follow you, all the painted boys die for you . . .' sang the young heroes of Poland. And kissing the lips and hands of their sweethearts, kneeling to receive the blessing of the Church, they flung themselves into the fire of war, in Poland first, and then on every front: North Africa, Normandy, Monte Cassino. In Poland itself in the first September days of war the cream of the cavalry did and dared and died in exploits which have become the stuff of legend.

If the cavalry, the Hussars, were imbued with all the romantic attributes of Polish pride, patriotism and nobility, no less were their horses. One proud laureate of pre-war horse-jumping, a splendid roan called Zbieg, refused to be harnessed to a supply wagon and tore himself from the traces with a huge leap, worthy of a gold medal. He later fell in battle, cut down by German artillery.[1]

Hussars, horses and *Harcerze* . . . Polish Boy and Girl Scouts would also play a significant part in the Polish resistance. The

1

Scout is 'the Polish Knight of old', declared a handbook printed by the wartime underground press, '. . . and the Girl Scout is no less worthy a sister of a Christian Knight. She follows the example of active and noble Polish gentlewomen.'[2]

Close links between Polish and Jewish Scouts kept vital lines of communication open. A Girl Scout leader, Maria Kann, wrote a brochure about the Warsaw Ghetto Uprising in 1943 which was the only publication in wartime Poland to deal exclusively with the events in the ghetto. However, it has to be said that one of the tenets of Polish Scouting was that 'non-Poles, and, above all, Jews' could not enter its ranks.

As the noose tightened around Warsaw in 1939 waves of bombers attacked the city. Buildings toppled, burying people in the ruins. Fires raged. On 14 September, the eve of Yom Kippur, the day of fasting and repentance, German planes bombed the predominately Jewish area of the city. It was an ominous sign and it seemed that the date was deliberately chosen.

A survivor who was seven at the time recalls, 'Mum and I held hands and we ran to Granny's – it had to be safer there! On the way I saw a house on fire on Gęsia (Goose) Street; fire exploded, sparks fell at my feet, the smoke suffocated me.'[3]

The relentless bombing continued. Roads out of Warsaw were blocked with people (including civic leaders) fleeing from the bombing. To add to the confusion, in response to the Nazi–Soviet secret agreement to carve up Poland, the Red Army crossed the eastern border. Polish soldiers were siphoned off to the USSR in wagonloads: many would perish in appalling conditions.

The following account comes from the memoir of Stanislaw Sznapman who lived in the Warsaw ghetto until July 1943. He wrote in hiding on the Polish side of the wall, where he died in unknown circumstances. Two Polish authors who had been actively involved in helping Jews in hiding preserved Stanislaw Sznapman's work.

'Monday, 25 September 1939 started with bombardment from the ground and from the air . . . Up till then we'd held ourselves together somehow, but that day everyone's nerves broke. People ran about madly, hiding in holes, shelters, cellars; others, gripped by deathly fear, ran about in panic not knowing where. Women lamented, children wept, praying aloud, kneeling on their doorsteps. On . . . 27 September, things became calm and at 12 noon it was announced that Warsaw had capitulated . . . Warsaw was left without water, electricity, gas or radios. The streets were choked with ruins and broken glass. The air was thick with dust and soot, but the population breathed again. People started to go out on to the streets to survey the devastation . . .'[4]

The devastation was indeed catastrophic. Thousands had died; bodies still lay in the streets. Twenty-five per cent of the city had been bombed and the most treasured historical monuments had been razed to the ground. In the New Order of the Nazis, Poles were to be the slaves of the Master Race and needed no history of their own. The next day, 28 September, the Germans ordered a detailed census of Warsaw's Jewish population. Older people, with memories of time spent in Germany before the war, of concerts and lectures and walks in the park, comforted themselves that there was nothing to worry about: Germans could be nothing else but civilized. However, it quickly became clear that this army had, as Sznapman puts it, turned back the clock of civilization a thousand years. His memoir continues:

'The regular German army began nightly raids on Jewish homes. The soldiers demanded jewellery and money at pistol point; they tortured and kicked the inhabitants. People who

dared lodge a complaint next day never saw the light of day
again . . . The Gestapo started to go mad . . . They began to
make planned and systematic tours of Jewish apartments and
took furniture, household equipment, linen. The owners were
required – under the threat of being beaten up – to carry their
own property down to the German vehicles outside. Doctors
were deprived of their instruments and microscopes . . . Jews
were required to give way to Germans on the streets and to
bow to them – and if anyone ignored this order they were
beaten and kicked until they were covered in blood . . . The
situation was so hopeless that the Germans were surprised that
there were so few suicides. But in our misery we were full of
optimism and hope that England and France would trample
into the dust this black plague which had choked all Europe . . .
We deluded ourselves that at any moment the situation would
change . . .'[5]

Young Nazi thugs mocked and ill-treated Orthodox Jews,
forcibly shaving, or painfully plucking out their beards.

In an interview with award-winning writer Hanna Krall, Dr
Marek Edelman, who was only 19 when he became one of the
inner command in the 1943 Uprising, says:

'I saw a public spectacle once on Żelazna (Iron) Street.
People were crowded around a barrel – an ordinary wooden
barrel, on which a Jew was standing. He was old, small and he
had a long beard. Beside him stood two German officers. (Two
handsome, grown men beside the round-shouldered Jew.) And
these Germans had huge tailor's scissors and were laughing
themselves silly as they cut off the old man's long beard bit by bit.

'The crowd was laughing too. Because objectively it was
really funny, a small guy on a wooden barrel with a beard that
was getting shorter and shorter, disappearing from sight
beneath those tailor's scissors. Like a comic scene in a film.

'There wasn't a ghetto yet, so there didn't seem to be anything threatening in the scene. After all nothing frightful was happening to the Jew: except that the soldiers could put him on that barrel without being punished; and people were already beginning to understand that there would be no punishment – and still it aroused their laughter.

'Do you know what? At that moment I understood that the most important thing of all is not to get pushed on to a barrel. Never, by no one. Do you understand? Everything I did after that was so that I wouldn't get pushed.'[6]

The Nazi plan was to concentrate Jews in major cities in Poland. Jewish Councils were set up to carry out Nazi decrees; in November 1939, only two months into the war, a command was given to the Jewish Council that the entire Jewish population of Warsaw would have to move into the confines of the mainly Jewish area. People were still in a state of deep shock after the initial bombing of Warsaw and the news of a ghetto caused great dismay, but the President of the Jewish Council, Adam Czerniaków, managed to stall Nazi plans. He notes in his diary: 'The establishment of a ghetto has been put back a few months. The Council is required to put up posters around the area with the warning "Epidemics – closed zone". Only through transit permitted.'[7]

On 23 November 1939 Jews were further discriminated against when the Nazis issued an order that from 1 December everyone over the age of ten must wear a white armband with a blue Star of David at all times on their outer clothing – the armbands had to be at least ten centimetres wide.

A survivor who was seven when war broke out recalls, 'They made us wear white bands with the Star of David. Mummy often hid her armband in her pocket. She considered this sign of discrimination degrading. It meant – we were different people, or, as the Germans said, quarter human. Father wore his band.'[8]

Adam Czerniaków, President of the Jewish Council, notes wryly: '1 December. A sleepless night. Took powder for headache . . . They brought the armbands with the Star of David to the office at 8 a.m. Well, in this way I've been given a new insignia . . .' and on 3 December he noted, 'This morning I went on foot through the town wearing the armband . . .'[9]

It must have weighed heavily on his arm! The factual comment voices no emotion but we hear the kind of stoical resignation typical of the 59-year-old engineer who had studied in Dresden and spoke good German. Czerniaków's unenviable position as puppet president inevitably brought him into conflict between the lethal demands of the Nazis and the enormous needs of the ghetto populace whose interests he tried vainly to represent.

That winter the snow fell heavily, shrouding sad remains of bombed out buildings. Struggling with cold, hunger, fear, people now branded with armbands slithered over icy pavements, passing the threatening notices. The new year, 1940, brought ever-increasing restrictions. On 1 January 1940 synagogues, prayer houses and ritual bath houses were closed. 'It's difficult to understand the point of this barbaric order,' noted Chaim Kaplan in his diary, *Scroll of Agony*. 'Is it really to do with fear of the spread of infectious diseases, or does the invader want to make life as unpleasant as possible for us?'[10]

On 13 January all Jewish males between the ages of 12 and 60 years were registered for forced labour, where they were subject to grim conditions and acts of mindless cruelty. The result was that many men hid at home and only women and children were seen on the streets.

'The endurance of women,' notes Emanuel Ringelblum at

the beginning of 1940. '. . . Women stand in long queues, hire themselves out to work. Gone are the elegant ladies, gone the elegant hats. Women work in the office and organise business. Women hold the home together. They queue for coal. Women are everywhere.'[11]

In February rationing was introduced. The amount of food per person per day was strictly calculated: 2,613 calories for Germans, 669 calories for Poles, 184 for Jews. Of course, it is impossible to survive on these low amounts, far less keep *kosher* requirements; and things were made worse by the constant influx of impoverished refugees who had been uprooted from outlying areas.

They came, cowed and disorientated, bowed beneath pathetic bundles, a new exodus: but this time there was no promised land, and no prophet with an outstretched arm to protect them, only the German guards whose delight was to degrade and terrify.

The incomers had been uprooted from cities and small towns of Poland where Jewish life had been firmly established for centuries. Many were already destitute and believed that in the capital city things would be safer – just as the little girl believed in the invincibility of Granny's house during the bombing.

The long queues of weary people quickly succumbed to hunger, disease and death. Rationing was so discriminatory, food prices so high that starvation was the order of the day and combating it became a way of resistance and protest. Soup kitchens were organized (some became centres for the young people who formed the Jewish underground) but the main victims of hunger were children.

Then at Easter, 1940 mob violence raged in Warsaw. In the wake of this, on 4 April 1940, a day, as he notes, of 'heavy leaden skies', the President of the Jewish Council, Adam Czerniaków, was summoned to the Gestapo and informed that the ghetto was to be walled off in order to protect the Jews! Jewish slave labour was used to build the walls. Every male was required to carry bricks to the site. Thus the Jews were compelled to build their own prison – and the Jewish Council was required to fund the materials.

Acts of gratuitous sadism continued. Even the President did not escape rough treatment. Two weeks before the ghetto was closed off Czerniaków was beaten up and imprisoned.

The President's experience was only too typical. Marek Stok, a lawyer, stressed the psychological pressure everyone was under: 'The feeling of being humiliated and abased never leaves you. The psychology of the slave is born – that's the first and worst result of the German rule.'[12]

Marek Stok also notes how the pressure built up.

'Towards the end of summer more and more evictions take place in the south of the city . . . it's now clear that there's going to be a ghetto behind the walls. The papers are full of advertisements about exchanging "Aryan" flats "within the walls" with Jewish ones "outside the walls". The din in the streets is incredible. Officially you're not allowed to bring in furniture, only hand luggage, but people break this rule and Germans turn a blind eye. So the streets are full of carts . . . loaded to the gunwales with goods and chattels, full too of people nervously rushing about, anxious to get into the area before the deadline.'[13]

There was a mad scramble for living space. Emanuel Ringelblum writes that the entire city of Warsaw was soon papered over with little white notices offering exchanges. He writes, 'Everyone is filled with a frightful feeling of uncertainty. Nobody knows what tomorrow will bring.'[14]

And, especially, nobody knew whether the ghetto was to be a 'closed' or 'open' one. Would they be allowed freedom of movement within the limited hours set for the stringent Jewish curfew – or would they be imprisoned within the ghetto walls? Nobody knew, and nobody was told.

On 16 November 1940 – significantly, the Jewish Sabbath – the walls were sealed and the gates in and out of the ghetto were guarded. Dr Ringelblum writes:

'Saturday, 16 November, the day they cut off the ghetto, was frightful . . . Streets are cut off from one another; you have to make detours. The streets are jam-packed, you can't get through, and pedestrians crowd the roads and pavements. A wave of cruelty has engulfed the whole city as if on an order given from above. People who don't raise their hats immediately they see a German are forced to do exercises with stones and bricks – even the elderly are made to do press-ups . . . An old man was going along the street and met two policemen. He didn't take off his cap and they tortured him for over an hour . . . Here's a Jewish family saying goodbye to their Polish friends. They kiss, wave, remind each other, "Come and see us next week . . ."'[15]

Marek Stok sums up the new situation: 'Jews are not allowed to go into the town and Aryans are not allowed to enter the ghetto. Stop. The die is cast. We are closed in. Now a new chapter of life begins. Life in the ghetto.'[16]

Notes

1 Zbieg's exploits are told in Bohdan Tomaszewski, *Horses and Riders: 70 Years of the Polish Union of Horse Riders*, Rzeczpospolita, 1998.

2 Gregorz Ciura, *To Do My Duty to God and Poland: Polish Scouts 1939–45*, ALFA Warsaw, 1998.

3 Alexandra Berłowicz in *Children*. My thanks to Ms Zak for permission to use this material.

4 *Memoirs.*

5 *Memoirs.*

6 Hanna Krall, *To Beat God to it!* (*Zdążyć przed Panem Bogiem*), Znak, Krakow, 1999. The English edition is translated as *To Steal a March on God*.

7 *Diary.*

8 Pola Elbinger in *Children*.

9 *Diary.*

10 Quoted in *Remnants*.

11 *Chronicle.*

12 *Memoirs.*

13 *Memoirs.*

14 *Chronicle.*

15 *Chronicle.*

16 *Memoirs.*

CHAPTER 2

Nightmare city

Living in the ghetto was like living with acute paranoia. The unimaginable became devastatingly real. Boundaries kept being changed: topography became fluid and unstable. What was known and trusted became perplexingly unattainable and daily life was full of such menace that it changed into a nightmare. It seemed unbelievable – but it was really happening. It was nightmare-like – but it was horrifyingly true.

An eyewitness comments: 'That same subconscious fear never left the people in the ghetto . . . and changed their lives into a nightmarish dream, when you feel with your whole being that something terrible is about to happen, only it's not clear yet what kind of danger threatens, nor where it comes from.'[1]

Fear, hunger, overcrowding, disease and death were direct and inescapable consequences of the creation of the Warsaw ghetto. Thousands of people had been displaced from their homes, from their jobs. And, as always in times of severe social change, there were 'dark characters', as some of the diarists call them, who exploited the new situation and became the *nouveau riche* among the prisoners in the ghetto.

Thousands of destitute people turned into walking skeletons whose flesh was as sparse as the rags tied around them. They took to the streets to beg; and ghetto dwellers felt their own humanity challenged as they witnessed the degradation and death of the needy.

'On the streets grown-ups and children died from hunger, cold and illness,' recalls Alexandra Berłowicz in the memoir of her childhood in the ghetto.

'Many – having sold their last stitch of clothing for money for food – wore only paper tied round with string. Papers held down with stones also covered the dead who lay in the streets because the undertakers, the Pinkert family, couldn't clear their corpses away quickly enough. I often saw funeral carts full to overflowing with the bodies of infants and older children. Sometimes it happened that families kept their dead at home for as long as they could so that they could use their ration cards even for a few more days . . .'[2]

President Adam Czerniaków writes, 'Now and again I write poetry. To do that you need a vivid imagination. Never has my imagination stretched so far that I can call the soup we give the populace a meal.'[3]

Samuel Puterman, a member of the newly created Jewish Police, wrote a memoir which vividly recreates life in those closed streets:

'A family from Łódź became very well known. At first it consisted of eight people. All they possessed in the world were two prams, in one of which he wheeled three children, while she pushed the other two along in the second. As they pushed the prams along the road they sang old Jewish songs. They had very nice voices. She sang, he joined in, and they were accompanied by eight distinct children's voices; then there were four, then three; and then one of the prams vanished, and so did their shoes and the rest of their outer clothing. Finally the family consisted of two people and one pram. So there they both were, he pushed the pram – and she lay inside it. She

12

was 39, but she looked like 100; she lay in the pram and sang duets with her husband. They sang the same songs and received the same few pence as last year.

'Another well-known character, who stood out from the grey mass of people dying against the walls of the buildings, was Nuchem Lejbkorn. Before the war he'd owned a house in one of the Warsaw suburbs, he'd had his own shop, a wife and five children. The Germans evacuated him to Warsaw. In a few months he became a beggar. At first the family lived in a sub-let room. Then his wife died of typhus. The oldest child died that same week. Nuchem and his four surviving children moved into a shelter for the homeless – and from there out on to the street. They walked around the streets . . . singing only one song in Yiddish . . . Then the children died of hunger, but he was still strong, he could still walk, although his legs were swollen. Autumn came, and he still kept going, but by winter he had no shoes, no clothes. All that remained was his feather quilt, so he went around in that, tied round with string in the middle. From the bottom of the quilt his monstrous swollen legs stuck out, from the top his small face with dried out yellow skin framed with a pointed beard. Feathers from his quilt scattered around him; and so passers by always gave him a wide berth, even in the overcrowded streets of the ghetto. Occasionally someone would throw a few pence into his tin and he seemed quite content. He meandered through the crowd with a smile on his lips – whether of an idiot or a wise man, and always sang the same little song . . .'[4]

Emanuel Ringelblum comments on the feathers, too. The bottom line of destitution, he noted, was when a person had nothing left except feathers – even the quilt cover had been sold for food.

'Hunger and poverty increased daily,' wrote an unnamed

woman who managed to escape from the ghetto with her four-year-old child towards the end of February 1943. She was actively involved in the struggle against hunger, working in the all-important 'house committees'. She also set up a soup kitchen which fed several hundred people every day. Her account continues:

'In the house where I lived there were 30 families (about 150 people) who needed care. They occupied a wooden out-building . . . There was no electric light, gas or water. Amongst the families in the wooden house were a cab driver whose horse had been taken by the Germans, a woman who sewed corsets and her two children; a teacher's widow from the provinces – he'd been murdered; some sort of bakery worker who had ten people to provide for. A dozen or more people took refuge in each flat: old parents, under-age children and young people who had been snatched from their place of work and were trying to scrape a bare existence by selling scraps of jumble on the street.'[5]

Marek Stok also records the appalling misery of the ghetto:

'Thousands of beggars simply make shift out in the street. They can no longer be called human, they're frightening apparitions, ghastly figures in filthy rags and tatters, legs swollen with hunger and emaciated faces with fevered eyes. They're everywhere, in the yards, on the pavements, under walls and on the roadway. They fight, shout, beg for alms. Children! The place is full of ragged children, who are almost naked despite the terrible frost. There's no way of shaking them off. You can't cross the street with food in your hand because some ragamuffin will run up, snatch the food and right there and then, as quickly as possible, starts to stuff bits of bread in his mouth, greedily. He's got to be as quick as he can because as soon as he grabs the bread from somebody and starts to stuff it

14

in his mouth, a whole pack of other ragged urchins pounce on
him, throw him to the ground and try to snatch the bread from
him. They roll on the road, fight, grabbing bits of bread from
each other and stuffing them down . . . You can't go any distance without coming across dead bodies . . . Shoot-outs and
murders never stop. A big car drives out along Karmelicka
Street and Leszno Street every day . . . Germans inside the car
shoot at pedestrians. There was a small sports car too, driven by
an officer. This 'gentleman' used to race at top speed in huge
zigzags along Leszno Street, simultaneously shooting pedestrians.
It was his way of having fun.'[6]

The ghetto inmates nicknamed one particularly bestial SS
man 'Frankenstein'. But the plight of the children aroused
horror and pity. Ringelblum notes that children as young as
three or four were reduced to begging – 'and that is the most
painful thing of all.' Here's his account of 14 November 1941:

'The first frosts have made themselves felt. People were
shivering with cold. Worst of all were the children freezing,
barefoot, bare legged, in rags, who stood silently crying. This
evening, 14 November, I heard the crying of just such a mite,
no more than three or four years old. We'll probably find his
frozen remains in the morning.'[7]

Ringelblum, who had devoted his life to social care, was
imprisoned in his room by the curfew which put the streets of
the ghetto absolutely out of bounds each night. He had to listen
to the distressed child without being able to help.

Another eyewitness describes a children's hospital:

'Children were lying on wooden bunks. They had no bedding, just mattresses made of paper . . . and on the boards were
skeletons – children, or enormous tumescent lumps. Only their
eyes were alive. If you've never seen those eyes, those faces of
starving children with open mouths like a black cave, with

wrinkled parchment skin, you do not know what life can be like.'[8]

Another author had first-hand experience of the ghastly harvest of death – he pushed one of the funeral carts. He writes:

'A mother is lying on a straw mattress with her son in his twenties. She's still alive, he died three days earlier. His body is as light as a feather. Gravediggers pick it up and carry it away to the cart. The mother doesn't even tremble. She doesn't even turn her head . . . The gravediggers swing their arms in a huge arc and toss this thing which was once a person as deep into the cart as possible so that he doesn't take up much room. There's no question of a coffin. The corpse lies in some kind of acrobatic position, with its head resting on the bottom of the cart, his back to the rear wall . . .'[9]

President Czerniaków notes in his *Diary*: '20 November 1941. Continual complaints that there's nothing to wrap corpses in. They will be buried naked in the ground. There isn't even any paper which as a last resort could have been used as a shroud.'[10]

It is the mark of civilization to surround death with respect, and the ghetto writers show their horror at this violation of human decency:

'Human remains are scattered into the pit like rubbish. There's a sound of the box being tipped out – and it's all over. An expression of shocked disgust comes over the faces of those present as though death was taking revenge for being deprived of its aura of mystery, of all the incidental trappings which surround it. Now, for spite, it has stripped itself naked, it has cast off its cerements – and there you have it. Look. It has totally exposed itself in all its nakedness before us all.'[11]

For many smuggling was the only way of survival – for others it brought death. An elderly lady has told me that her mother baked a cake and left the ghetto with her youngest child, a little boy, to try to sell it. Neither was ever seen again. This lady survived because she escaped to the Soviet Union. Her sister in the Warsaw ghetto owed her survival to Polish families who hid her.

Smuggling happened on a vast scale. Some smugglers were professionals who made enormous fortunes, thousands were simply children who risked their lives as they crept through drains and gaps in the wall to bring back food for their families. People were particularly moved by the heroism of starving children who risked their lives for their families. The children never tried to satisfy their own hunger with the food they carried home. Jack Eisner, a Holocaust survivor, honoured them in his moving memorial to child victims of the Holocaust in the Jewish Cemetery in Warsaw. He writes:

'It was in this very cemetery that I learnt how to survive, along with my group of juvenile smugglers. Everything is just where it always was – the tree with the letter Z carved on it was the place where we used to meet . . . Only I am not the same any more. Only there is still a "me". Only I am the one who survived.'[12]

Jack Eisner's memorial consists of a reconstruction of the ghetto wall with photographs of children and plaques with a poignant reminder: 'Granny Masha had 20 grandchildren, Granny Hana had 11. Only I survived.' Opposite is part of a poem in honour of child smugglers. This poem made an enormous impression in the ghetto; everyone quoted it. Emanuel Ringelblum records hearing the poet recite her own work:

'25 August 1941: Henryka Lazowertówna recited verses she'd composed in honour of smugglers. In the struggle with thugs, with Jewish, Polish and German police, they display a truly extraordinary courage. These youngest smugglers deserve especial sympathy; like so many rats, they get through the drainage system beside the gates. There's just no way to describe how much courage they have in getting across to the other side where Polish police or petty criminals torment them. Often the guards confiscate all their smuggled goods. A few weeks ago I witnessed the following scene: a little boy was weeping on the corner of Chłodna (Cool) and Żelazna (Iron) Streets, tearing his hair out and shaking as if he had a high temperature. He looked beseechingly at the guard who had grabbed his bag. The child's weeping had no effect on the heartless gendarme . . . The little smuggler commemorated by the poet represents thousands of four- and five-year-old child smugglers who risk their lives several times a day providing food for themselves and for the Jewish population.'[13]

Henryka Lazowertówna (1910–42) had published two collections of poems in the Polish language and was known as a promising young poet. Polish friends offered her shelter and a chance of escape but she refused to leave her mother and they both perished in Treblinka. Henryka took an active part in Oneg Shabat. Her work spoke directly to the hearts of her audience. Thousands of people visit the Jack Eisner memorial each year and read the extract of her famous poem, *Little Smuggler*, which is carved there.

> Little smuggler
> Across walls, through holes and guard posts,
> Over wire, across ruins, fences and gates,
> Hungry, dare-devil, stubborn,
> I slip by, race through like a cat . . .
> And if the hand of fate all of a sudden
> Reaches me sometime in this game,
> That's just what commonly happens,

So, Mummy, don't expect me at home . . .
And only one single worry fixes
My face in a frown:
Who will bring bread tomorrow
To Mummy if I don't return?[14]

Here's the voice of a child smuggler, Marysia Szpiro. She wrote her memoir in 1946, when she was 11.

'At first my sister Dora and my brother Josek (smuggled) because I was too little. Mummy went to the guard post to help them get out. Sometimes they had to stand there all day without managing to get across. When they did get across and came home with the "loot" and a German caught them – he took everything. That was the worst because then mummy didn't have any more money for food. But there were days when Dora and Josek came home with food. Later I started to go across to the other side as well. I was so small no one paid any attention to me. There was this hole in the fence and I put the things there. Sometimes I had to wait for a long time because I couldn't get back into the ghetto. If the policeman was cruel he caught the children and beat them until they were bleeding all over . . . There was one policeman, though, and when he was on duty I could go across the wall and back as many times as I needed. The children who wouldn't get through to the other side suffered terribly from hunger. They lay there on the streets in rows, living and dead children.'[15]

Rela Sapot, who was hidden by a Polish friend, witnessed a policeman shoot dead a little girl of about ten who was smuggling a parcel into the ghetto. On 1 July 1942, as Rela was escaping from the ghetto for good, she got through to the Polish side of the wall. A German officer arrested a little boy who had a small sack of potatoes. The officer ordered passers-by to open a manhole cover into the sewer and throw the child in. When no one would obey this order, the officer opened the cover himself and tossed the little boy to his death.[16]

Now, as we see elderly men stand in the dock hundreds of miles from the scene of their crimes, I wonder where the officer is who murdered a starving child that day. Did he survive the war and play with his children and grandchildren?

Three weeks later the ghetto children were murdered by the Master Race.

Notes

1 Władyslaw Szpilman, *Death of the Town* (*Śmierć miasta*), 1946, quoted in *Survive!* Szpilman's book has been translated into English as *The Pianist* (Gollancz, London, 1999).
2 *Children.*
3 *Diary.*
4 *Memoirs.*
5 *Memoirs.*
6 *Memoirs.*
7 *Chronicle.*
8 Adina Blady-Szwager, in *Remnants.*
9 Quoted in *Text.*
10 *Diary.*
11 Lejb Goldin, *Chronicle of a Single Day*, quoted in *Text.*
12 Quoted in Jan Jagielski, *Guide to the Jewish Cemetery in Warsaw*, Book 1 (Tow. Opieki nad zabytkami, Warsaw, 1996).
13 *Chronicle.*
14 Quoted in *Guide* (note 12 above).
15 *Memoirs.*
16 Rela's story is narrated in *Memoirs.*

CHAPTER 3

Bridges to nowhere

On 26 January 1942 a wooden bridge was put up by Jewish slave labour to link the large and the small ghetto because the Germans needed a through road for transport. The bridge was for pedestrians only. It became a symbol of oppression for the prisoners inside the ghetto.

Dr Jan Leociak of Warsaw University has studied the Holocaust archives of the Jewish Historical Institute. He writes:

'In the traditional concept of space a bridge is a positive symbol. It allows us to surmount a precipice or uncontrollable sources of water. It increases the possibility of moving around; it creates greater comfort. It's a sign of victory over elements which conspire against us. It joins two banks, two edges and creates common space – a space of meeting. We imagine a bridge above all as something which joins two sundered parts into one whole, enabling the conquest of the thing which divides us. For the inhabitants of the Warsaw ghetto the bridge lost that positive worth. It was a spectacular proof that they found themselves in some absurd spatial position. It reminded them of the humiliating situation of being shut in. It affirmed that there was a great separation between the ghetto and the rest of the world . . .'[1]

One writer called the bridge, 'a monument to the miseries of hundreds of thousands of people,' and another referred to it as 'an urban wound on the face of Warsaw.'[2]

21

A poet tells his son:

'Every time I climb up on to the bridge and back down the other side, I ask God that this wooden bridge of theirs would break apart into tiny pieces. Perhaps it's because of the soldiers in their helmets who stand underneath with grins on their faces, mocking the monkey-like people who swarm across the bridge. And perhaps it's because the bridge is dreadfully dirty, covered in mud, so we're up to our ankles in mire. Maybe as well because only Jews weave their way across the bridge, that the bridge teems with shame from these armbands like grave-cloths. It is their bridge . . . Don't drag me over bridges which are bound to collapse one day. I shall stay alive and show you how their accursed bridge will burst and fall to bits.'[3]

A member of the Jewish Police, Jan Mawult, writes: 'Thousands of lowered heads are raised to greet the panorama . . . the crosses on the churches and the line of the distant Vistula. With a sigh heads are bowed once more. The ghetto bridge is the Ponte di Sospiri, the Bridge of Sighs.'[4]

Shifting boundaries, walls cutting off familiar streets, a bridge from nowhere to nowhere, crowds packed closely together all day every day, death a daily occurrence: this was life in the ghetto. To add to the confusion bewildered people displaced from other European countries were constantly arriving and needing to be housed. Then, late in 1941, young couriers, who risked their lives smuggling information between the beleaguered Jewish communities of Poland, brought the Warsaw ghetto news about mass murders by Nazi killing squads near Vilnius. And early in 1942, reports began to filter through of mass murder in Chełmno, about 50 km from the industrial city of Łódź, alarmingly close at hand. An empty castle in forestland had been equipped for mass murder – and this was simply too shocking to be believed.

Although the German leadership intended to keep their crimes totally secret, the horrifying news leaked out. Three men who had been employed as gravediggers escaped from the camp at Chełmno. On 27 January 1942 a woman called Fela broke the news in a letter to her family in the Warsaw ghetto:

'My dears! I've already written a postcard to you about the fate which has befallen us. You see, they transported us to Chełmno and gassed us. 25,000 Jews lie there already. The slaughter is still continuing. Don't you pity us? Natan, our child and mother and I escaped. Nobody else. What will happen to us from now on I don't know, I have no strength left to live . . .'[5]

The reaction in Warsaw was sheer disbelief. 'The Warsaw ghetto didn't believe the news,' wrote Marek Edelman, whose memoir of the Ghetto Uprising was published in 1945. Marek Edelman was a teenage member of a socialist movement, the Bund; he highlights the role his organization played in the resistance within the ghetto.

'All those people who were clinging on to life couldn't believe that life could be taken from them like that. Only the young people of the youth organizations, carefully observing the gradual growth in German terror, acknowledged that these cases were probable and true and decided to organize a wide propaganda campaign to raise people's consciousness.'[6]

Other members of the Ringelblum Archive took the news seriously too, and newspapers verifying the information began to circulate throughout the ghetto.

Yet life went on. The synagogues were shut but cantors sang prayers in the street. Emanuel Ringelblum notes that Hasidic Jews still danced before the Lord as they used to do before the war. They put up a big poster, 'Don't lose hope!' However, many rabbis preferred not to endanger themselves or their families by active opposition to Nazi decrees. Ringelblum notes that the concept of 'Kiddush Hashem' – blessing the Holy Name of God – had been sublimated into a simple struggle to survive (23 March 1941). Yiddish culture, however, enjoyed a new level of interest and Ringelblum and other ghetto writers mention 'intensive cultural activity': underground colleges and libraries flourished. Many young people, among them future members of the Jewish Fighting Force, taught children by day and met together to study by night. Newspapers were printed and young people, especially girls in their teens and twenties, acted as couriers at great risk to themselves. Polish Scouts, girls and boys, helped the young couriers. A nun who worked for the underground near Vilnius sheltered some of the resistance workers. She wrote fondly of them:

'They were peaceful and resigned . . . many had lost their nearest and dearest – these last were even more peaceful, even more silent, only pain was hidden in their eyes . . . They called me "mother". I felt as though I really were. The arrival of each new member of their group encouraged me, I was grieved that I couldn't give refuge to more. I remember them still today. Maybe I loved these last ones the most. My little girls: Tauba – who loved life so much, serene and sweet, she nevertheless had the courage as a partisan to throw a grenade at a German vehicle and perish heroically. Margalit – weeping for her marriage as she worked in the kitchen. Sarenka K – a delicate and loving mother who valiantly bore the death of her husband and the pain of being parted from her child. Chuma – active and energetic, a hard-working young girl whose stability and wisdom acted soothingly on everyone around her. Witka – a liaison worker with the ghetto – she laid mines on the nearby tracks . . .'[7]

Ringelblum's *Chronicle* praises the young women whose

24

involvement in pre-war youth movements had led them into active participation in the resistance movements:

'The brave girls, Chajka, Frumka and others deserve the pen of a great writer: these courageous, heroic girls travel out from the ghetto to the cities and small towns of Poland. They have "Aryan" documents as Poles or Ukrainians. One of them even wears a little cross from which she's never parted – she really feels the lack of it when she's in the ghetto! Day after day they are exposed to the greatest dangers. They depend entirely on their Aryan looks, on the scarves with which they cover their heads. They undertake the most dangerous tasks without a word of protest, without a moment's hesitation . . . Nothing is difficult for them, nothing stands in their way. How many times have they looked death in the eyes! How many times have they been arrested, searched! None the less good fortune has accompanied them. Emissaries of a good cause are invulnerable to danger. With what simplicity and modesty they report back about the things they've achieved . . . Jewish women have inscribed a beautiful page in the deeds of Jews in the present world war. Chajka and Frumka take the main place in that history (19 May 1942).'[8]

Music, art, poetry were a means of resistance too. A girl of 18, Maria, or Marysia, Ajzensztadt, was called 'the nightingale of the ghetto'. Her singing transported her listeners to worlds far away from the horror and fear of their everyday lives. Although Jews were forbidden to sing or play music by non-Jewish composers, Marysia defied the censors. Ringelblum writes: 'Marysia gave concerts in cafés as well as at social gatherings with her repertoire in Polish, Hebrew and Yiddish. Her performances brought an atmosphere of purity and art to various places of entertainment often of doubtful repute.'[9]

For there was, of course, a shady side to ghetto life.

Corruption was rife. Smuggling netted vast fortunes for the ghetto 'mafia' who threw their newly acquired money around and held wild parties to which the Gestapo were also invited. It's thought that many of the *nouveau riche* of the ghetto had been small-time dealers and porters who had struggled to make ends meet in the immediate pre-war years. Victims of stringent anti-Semitism before the war, they now rose to the top of the claustrophobic, fearful, unstable world of the ghetto. With the smell of death in the air, the 'good life' had a desperate tinge. 'Eat, drink and be merry for tomorrow we die' became an alternative philosophy for adults and young people alike. This turned out too to be a bridge which led to nowhere. The main beneficiaries of the new order were the smuggling bosses – particularly a group called the 'Thirteen' – and the Jewish Police.

The 'Thirteen' – so called because their headquarters was at 13 Leszno Street – were a group of protectionists and Gestapo agents who amassed great fortunes from bribes and blackmail and spread a network of terror within the ghetto. At their head was a man called Gancwajch. In his effort to gain control over the ghetto, Gancwajch made a show of philanthropy. Ringelblum notes, 'Gancwajch is a fascinating speaker and thanks to this he gains followers who don't know about his dirty machinations. They believe he might achieve something, especially when he makes it known that he might be able to help in the area of supplies . . .'[10]

The theme of Gancwajch's powerful speeches was that the Jews would be safe if they collaborated with the Nazis. This was certainly a bridge which led to nowhere – and was never part of the mind-set of people in the ghetto. Even though it became increasingly clear that Jewish life was doomed to extinction everyone remained deeply convinced that Nazism would fail in the end.

A pair of Gestapo agents who became an institution in the ghetto were two refugees from the Łódź ghetto, Kohn and Heller. In the topsy-turvy values of the doomed Jewish quarter, smuggling which brought wealth to a few also benefited the population as a whole; similarly the initiatives of Kohn and Heller, who ran a taxi service with horse-drawn cabs, made them a useful, if ambiguous, part of ghetto life.

The main organization, however, which was to become hated and feared by everyone, was seen at first in a positive light. This was the Jewish Service of Protection and Order: the Jewish Police.

The Jewish Police were unarmed and unpaid, which immediately laid them open to corruption. A high proportion of lawyers and university graduates joined. They hoped they might be able to protect themselves and their families by serving the Germans – in the end this too proved a bridge which led them nowhere.

At first people believed that a police force made up of their own kind would be merciful – but events proved otherwise. Jan Mawult, a member of the police force, writes:

'If the reader, scanning these pages, had lived in the Warsaw ghetto in those days, he would certainly . . . ask, "Why did these people turn out to be so bad, why did they do so much evil against the populace, why did the populace hate them so much?" Let the reader hold back from pronouncing judgement . . . let him become acquainted with the real state of affairs . . . and let him try once again, for the hundredth time, for the thousandth time to get to the bottom of the reality we had to live with.'[11]

Mawult justifies the way the police demanded bribes. 'Bribes *had* to exist in the ghetto, they were an inescapable fulfilment of an unhealthy, incorrect and unjust reality.'[12]

A different view comes from an engineer, Henryk Bryskier: '. . . the Jewish Police organization was amoral in its very foundation . . . The character and circumstances of the Force quickly depraved the majority of these "honorary" workers.'[13]

If the Jewish Police became known for corruption, Dr Janusz Korczak was already a legendary hero in his own right. His altruism and self-sacrifice challenged and inspired people in the ghetto – and long afterwards. A paediatrician, Dr Korczak had also devoted his life to children's literature and broadcasting. He was a director of orphanages for both Polish and Jewish children. In the children's homes, as well as in his writings, Dr Korczak empowered children. In his orphanages there were regular consultations, 'parliaments' in which children had equal right to evaluate their teachers and award them good and bad marks. Similarly his books show children in control of situations which baffle adults.

In an early work, written in 1904, the hero is none other than St Nicholas himself, who goes in disguise through the poor streets of Warsaw:

'I go from hut to hut – an old grey-haired man for whom the centuries are years.

'Snow sparkles with diamonds in the twinkling worlds of the stars. I feel the movement of these star-giants, of the earth spinning without rest, as if nothing were happening upon it.

'And I see guilt, but I do not see guilty people. I see injury and crime but I do not see criminals.

'I walk with tears in my heart and with God on my lips.'[14]

Those words sum up Korczak himself. On a visit to London in 1911 he had actually vowed himself to a single life in the service of children. He wrote: 'A slave has no right to have children . . . For my son I chose the idea of serving the child and his concerns.'[15]

When the war came and the ghetto walls began to rise people said confidently, 'They won't touch Korczak's children.' But his orphanage was swept into the ghetto. 'Then let us save you at least,' his Polish friends begged. 'Can you save the children?' Dr Korczak asked. 'Alas, no, there are too many. . .' 'Then I shall go into the ghetto with my children,' the doctor replied.

Hating the discriminatory politics which differentiated between people, Dr Korczak refused to wear the obligatory armband. He was arrested and incarcerated in the notorious Pawiak prison, returning shaken and fearful. But his efforts on behalf of his children were heroic. Despite the starvation in the ghetto no child in Dr Korczak's care suffered hunger. He was helped by his friend and assistant, Stefania Wilczyńska, whose unflagging dedication was recalled by one of the young people under her care:

'Miss Stefa used to spend the whole day with us. She got up before us and was the last person to go to sleep; even when she was ill she didn't stop work . . . Tall, in a black apron, her hair cut short like a man's, she was always attentive and watchful . . . The house was full of Miss Stefa, we felt her thoughtfulness, her care everywhere.'[16]

And if the house was 'full of Miss Stefa', out in the streets, clad in the Polish army officer greatcoat which he had worn in the First World War, was the 67-year-old doctor, tirelessly begging food for his children. As he struggled through the overcrowded ghetto, a sack flung over one shoulder, he stopped to comfort abandoned and dying children, lifting them from the pavement into empty shops or bombed out homes and sitting with them until they died.

Thinking back over his life, he noted a moment from his childhood in his ghetto diary: the death of his pet canary.

'Its death had raised the secret problem of religious belief. I had wanted to put a cross on its grave. The maid said, no, because it was only a bird, something less than a person. It was even a sin to cry.

'So much for the maid, but it was worse when the janitor's son pronounced that the canary was a Jew.

'And so was I.

'I was a Jew too, while he was a Pole, a Catholic. He would go to heaven while I, if I don't say any ugly words and obediently bring him sugar stolen from the house – I shall receive after death something which isn't exactly hell, but it's dark there. And I was afraid of being alone in the dark.

'Death – Jew – hell. A black, Jewish paradise. That was something to puzzle out.'[17]

On 4 August 1942, two days before he walked across the terrain of the ghetto for the last time with the children from his orphanage, Janusz Korczak wrote:

'I was watering the flowers, the poor orphanage plants, the plants of a Jewish orphanage. The baked earth sighed.

'A sentry was watching my work. Does it annoy him, does it sadden him, this domestic work of mine at six o'clock in the morning?

'He stands and watches. He positions his legs astride.

'. . . I don't wish anyone evil. I don't know how to. I don't know how it is done.

'I am watering plants. My bald head shines in the windows – what a good target!

'He's got a machine gun. Why does he stand and watch so peacefully?

'He hasn't received any orders.

'Or perhaps in civilian life he was a village schoolmaster, perhaps a notary, or a street cleaner in Leipzig, a waiter in Cologne?

'What would he do if I nodded to him? Would he greet me with a friendly wave of his hand?

'Perhaps he doesn't even know that things are as they are?

'Perhaps he arrived only yesterday from somewhere far away...'[18]

Perhaps... but he has come to do harm, to steal the lambs from the fold, to drive children into the valley of the shadow of death. Janusz Korczak, their good shepherd, will walk with them. Will there be green pastures for ghetto children, sparkling water, rainbows, flowers, verdant places for endless play?

Notes

1 *Text.*
2 Quoted in *Text.*
3 Quoted in *Remnants.*
4 Quoted in *Text.*
5 *Letters.*
6 *The Ghetto is Fighting.*
7 Anna Borkowska in *Homeland.*
8 *Chronicle.*
9 *Chronicle.*
10 *Chronicle.*
11 *Memoirs.*
12 Quoted by Tomasz Grosse in *Survive!*
13 *Survive!*
14 Quoted in Krystyna Staszewska, *The religious consciousness of Janusz Korczak* in Hanna Kirchner, *Janusz Korczak – Writer, Educator, Philosopher* (*Pisarz, wychowawca myśliciel*), IBL, Warsaw, 1997.
15 Quoted in Piotr Matywiecki, *The Spiritual and Actual Journey of*

J.K. to Palestine, in Kirchner, *Janusz Korczak – Writer, Educator, Philosopher.*

16 Ida Merzan, quoted in Jan Jagielski, *Guide to the Jewish Cemetery in Warsaw*, Tow. Opieki nad zabytkami, Warsaw, 1996.

17 Quoted in *Martyrdom and Extermination of the Jews (Męczeństwo i Zagłada Żydów)*, ed. Irena Maciejewska, Krajowe Agencje Wydawnicza, Warsaw, 1988.

18 Quoted in *Martyrdom and Extermination of the Jews.*

CHAPTER 4

'The decree is sealed . . .'

'On the First Day of the Year it is inscribed, and on the Day of Atonement the decree is sealed, how many shall pass away, and how many shall be born, who shall live and who shall die . . .' These words were sung at Rosh Hashanah in the year which would see more than 300,000 people 'pass away' from the Warsaw ghetto. Despite the suffering in the ghetto people kept the feasts as best they could. Rabbi Szymon Huberband, a member of the archive group, Oneg Shabat, noted: 'There was no oil for the Hanukah lamps. The menorah was hidden, we couldn't set lit candles in our windows as Jewish law prescribes: people were too afraid.'[1]

The unthinkable kept happening. Reduced to starvation, people sold even their most sacred possessions: the holy books, prayer shawls and leather tefilim (personal boxes containing the Law) – all essential items for Jewish religious observance. Rabbi Huberband noted sadly:

'Prayer shawls are dyed in different colours and sewn up as women's dresses. These dyed shawls are sold in various markets, shopping halls and bazaars . . . Tefilim are sold at ridiculously low prices, poverty in the ghetto is so enormous that Jews sell tefilim and the Books of the Torah for a few pence.'[2]

Almost inevitably the practice of religion weakened along with family ties and with the growth of corruption in a society which had been put under unimaginable pressure. People were

forced to work on holy days. Bathhouses were closed – though
four still functioned in strict secrecy.

Ringelblum's *Chronicle* also comments on the sale of holy
books. 'An unprecedented spectacle! Talmudic books used to be
sacred and were passed down from generation to generation.
Selling these books on the street is a real insult to God and
shows the degree of the current decline (in religion).'[3]

Ringelblum notes how wide-ranging interests were despite
the close confines of the ghetto.

'January 1942: There are no Jewish bookshops. They've all
been closed and the books were confiscated . . . But books are
now sold quite openly on the streets. There's no lack of forbidden goods like the works of Feuchtwanger, Zweig, Lenin,
Marx and others, even openly anti-Nazi literature . . . Foreign
language books are hugely popular, especially books in English
(published by Penguin). People are keen to study because
they're getting ready to emigrate after the war.'[4]

This remark shows how even informed people had no idea
that the Warsaw ghetto was doomed to be totally exterminated,
even though postcards from other ghettos kept arriving by the
official post, and letters were smuggled in, alarming the Warsaw
ghetto underground. These poignant missives are all that is left
of the senders – and the addressees. Stored in the Ringelblum
Archive, and recently collected in a book by Dr Ruta Sakowska,
these letters express the inexpressible. They report, sometimes
obliquely, often in code, facts about mass extermination which
the Nazi perpetrators were trying at all costs to hide. This alone
gives them a unique importance. In them we hear the voice
not of the makers, but of the victims of history. They are the
voice of the powerless – and this above all explains their
special drawing-power. So little survived the wreckage of the
Holocaust: shoes, drawings, photographs, human hair – and

these letters. Written in Yiddish, or transliterated into Latin characters, in Polish or in ungrammatical, broken Polish with many spelling mistakes, in and of themselves they have no special literary value. And yet their erroneous orthography makes them all the more authentic. They are the echoes of a vanished people – but if we listen carefully, these voices speak more poignantly, more powerfully than any historian – though we need the historian's guiding hand to understand the barely-breathed allusions, to trace the family tree, to outline and underline, as Dr Sakowska does in her book, so that private letters have real documentary worth.

Here are a few extracts from this remarkable correspondence.

The first come from Roza Kaplan. Hearing of mass exterminations in Chełmno, on 20 January 1942 Roza wrote to warn relatives in Warsaw:

'And now dear Hela, as I told you, Mela and Samek are in Gostyninie, and they did well, because if not, they would be here, where your Father, Uncle David Taube senior, and his wife and everyone are . . . they are all there in the place where Uncle David went . . . This is worse than the plague, and if we see each other again it will be a Divine miracle. *Shma Israel* was on everyone's lips. Their *kysa* (perishing) was frightful. Oh, that we had never been born! Dear David, I know I am causing you great pain, but you have to know, this is a cry from a hurting heart. My dear Hela and David, be brave and try to keep well, because now only you are left . . .'[5]

Roza had met one of the escapees who brought back news of the exterminations at Chełmno. She wrote to her husband on 21 January 1942:

'My darling! I'm in such a mood that I shouldn't be writing to you. I know that it will be bad for your health – I'm sorry for you, my dear, but every letter I write I think this is my

last . . . I've just spoken to someone who's arrived from
Chełmno (Roza misspells it *Chelmio*) . . . I can't go back to you
(in Warsaw) because it's winter, so spread the word, perhaps
these people (in Warsaw) will help me so that I don't suffer and
leave this world in such a tragic way. Forgive me for writing
like this, you'll think I'm being hysterical. Oh, if only it were
all a lie!'[6]

And the next day Roza continues:

'This story has broken us terribly and especially me. I can't
work, I cry all day, I'm terribly sorry for my children – why
did I give birth to them? Don't think that what I wrote to you
was a load of cobblers. That procedure doesn't stop. Full wagons
go from Łódź in the same direction every day . . . although it's
quiet here, no one sleeps at night . . .'[7]

Three days later she writes:

'We're still here for the time being . . . They've been looking for them (the escapees). At the same time they (the Nazi
leaders) promise that it won't happen to this district and that
we'll be here until April . . . I don't know what else to do
except to sit and wait. Maybe now people know about it, this
illness (mass murder) will stop . . . It's just too bad that we
already know what is in store for us. It's better not to know and
then it's a surprise, so even when you're being deported, you
still think you'll sort something out somehow . . .

'27 January 1942 . . . I fasted today for the second time in
the course of one week. Even little Jerzyk didn't eat anything
either. Yes, my dear, a drowning person clutches a straw. Maybe
it will help. We're more depressed than I can say. The *shechita*
(slaughter) continues. It's become very much talked about.
Those guests who returned from the other world – they
looked for them here. Don't think it's all a made-up fairy tale.
I can't work, I'm so out of sorts and resigned. I oughtn't to

think so much about it, but I can't get a grip of myself . . .

'30 January 1942 . . . I felt as though I were drowning. Unfortunately I still haven't calmed down completely . . . after all, as long as your eyes are open you can't really believe that this is going to happen to us . . . Our lad's sprouted like an oak, in normal times our hearts would be bursting with pride that we've got three boys like oaks . . . I fasted for the third time yesterday, like at Yom Kippur. I've become pious and day after day I ask God to grant us life, because that's our one desire . . .'[8]

In February Roza writes to her brother and sister-in-law:

'Write how things are with you – it will be easier for me if I knew that you're all right at least . . . From your postcard I realize that you know about everything . . . and so you can imagine our mood – the waiting – many times I feel ready for anything – afterwards comes a wave of protest – why – I don't want to perish like that, or my nearest and dearest. Even little Chaimek says he doesn't want to go to Uncle David . . .'[9]

Roza's last letters were written on 20 February to her husband and 22 February to her brother. In her letter to her husband she explains that everyone in the ghetto is being required to pay 8 marks per head for the deportation costs – an ominous sign that the end is at hand. She writes:

'The first dance began here yesterday, and that's 8 marks per head . . . that's more than 7,000 (Polish zloties) from our poor ghetto . . . I don't know what to do. Should I leave – it's below zero, if I don't go – I'm still going to lose. What should I do? . . . If only we could see each other once again . . .'[10]

Another letter, written by an unidentified man to his friend in Warsaw, describes the deportation of another community to the Chełmno extermination camp:

'Dear friend! Joseph's wife asked me to write to you, and to

father above all, that Joseph and Alter from Zychlin are ill. It's
the same illness which Joseph the Righteous suffered from for
twelve years (Genesis 37—40). They are in great need of
Divine mercy. All Jews need mercy very much. I've already said
farewell to you many times and yet maybe dear God will save
us. This morning Josef Princ died just like lightning. They shot
him in the face. On Sunday Iccak Kubic's daughter-in-law
died in the street. Abram Rozenberg's sister died from the same
illness as well.

'What's new with you? May you live to see the liberation!
And now about us. You know that our days are numbered.
There's no guard, no protection . . . We have been thrown into
the jaws of fate. And now, my dears, you know what my name
is. If I stay alive – that's good; and if not, then you must pray to
God for my soul. The books of commentaries are in the cellar
beside the south wall.

'I bow to you all and wish you health. My family greets
you. I'm not broken, thank God, because, after all, everything
comes from the dear Creator. Only may I not doubt at the last
moment. I ask for your forgiveness.'[11]

As 1942 wore on, more letters and postcards arrived warning
of mass murder in other parts of Poland.

A man writes to a friend in Warsaw about the loss of his
nearest and dearest:

'Unfortunately there's no one left to buy birthday presents
for. Two days ago before our little Sunshine's birthday we lost
our dearest parents and darling Pepka and sweetest little
Imeczka. I'm left with Dudek. We're alone in our pain and
despair. There's no consolation for us . . . Their death was
dreadful. Together with 2,000 of our brothers and sisters. In a
common grave. There has never been such a *shechita* (slaughter)
anywhere before. They didn't spare pregnant women, tiny

children, the elderly. Blood poured in torrents . . . But now our pain and despair grow with every day, every moment. I can in no way reconcile myself to the thought that they're lost. I shut my eyes and I see them in front of me. I have little Imeczka's tinkling laugh continually in my ears . . .

'Pepka, boundlessly giving of herself and self-sacrificing, happy if she could do someone a good turn . . . The child meant everything to her, part of her life, and with her own eyes she had to watch the death of her little son. Clinging to his mother's neck – they both fell into the grave . . . I don't believe in anything now, there can be no Providence if it can come to this, that such pure, innocent beings went like sheep to the slaughter . . . The feeling of powerlessness is what torments me most. We are just cattle, we must wash, get dressed, eat . . . No, there's no consolation for me now. I haven't got a heart inside me, only a stone, otherwise it would have burst long ago. Sometimes I tell myself that I must bear it like a man so that I can avenge them when the right time comes, but these are just words. Everything is empty. Nothing can bring my loved ones back to me again.

'Be well, dear friend and don't think badly of me because I've been sharing my pain. You knew my dear ones so well that I had to write to you about them . . . Be well and remember this: the most important, most realistic thing for you and your mother is to prepare a hiding place inside your own home . . .'[12]

The information put so poignantly and cryptically in these letters and postcards was published by the underground press; the news was also smuggled out of the ghettos to the Polish underground. But it was a letter in June 1942 which shook the ghetto underground rigid – it warned them in code that the extermination camp at Treblinka was almost ready.

'. . . Uncle is planning (God preserve us) to hold a wedding for his children also at your place too (God forbid); he's rented a place for himself near you, really close to you, and you probably don't know a thing about it, that's why I'm writing to you and I'm sending a special messenger with this letter, so that you'll be informed about it. It's true and you must rent new places outside the town for yourselves and for all our brothers and sons of Israel. Because he has already prepared new homes for you all, just like he had by us (Sobibor). Perhaps you didn't know about this at all. That's why I'm writing especially to you so you'll hear about it, because uncle is planning to banish Adam (Hebrew – all humankind). And, please God, you won't find yourselves alongside Shlome Wewel of blessed memory. We know for sure that uncle has got this place almost ready for you. You must know about it, you must find some way out. You've got to know about it, uncle is planning, God forbid, to hold this wedding as soon as possible, and he's got the place already, right close beside you. Remember about those new places. Go into hiding – that's the best medicine for this illness. Remember – we are holy sacrifices, "and if some is left till morning" etc.'[13]

This last sentence was the give-away. It referred to the instructions for the Passover in Exodus 12.10: any leftovers from the sacrificial lamb *had to be burnt*. The people in the underground knew immediately what was meant. Emanuel Ringelblum notes: 'Letters from Włodawa about the bonfire and executioner's stake being prepared close by Warsaw.'[14]

Passover 1942 in the Warsaw ghetto was muted. Everyone was grieving. Samuel Puterman, a member of the Jewish Police, recorded the event:

'The second Passover in the ghetto. There was probably not a single family in the ghetto whose members had not been

felled by death. The first night of Seder. The festival of remembrance. Families gathered around tables spread with white
cloths. They repeated the words of the *Hagadah* mechanically.
What did the fate of their brothers centuries ago mean to
them? Last year Father had still been alive, mother, brothers,
sisters, husbands had been there. At the Traubes' the same white
tablecloth which was meant for 24 people was folded in
two . . . Fela is a widow now. She is sitting with her little
daughters. Mother and daughters secretly wipe tears from their
eyes. Everyone is weeping. Jakub Traube heroically fights back
tears in his throat. He can't sing the words of the *Hagadah* any
more. He lost his brother two months ago. He had been walking
along Karmelicka Street. A German car drove up, carrying
prisoners to the Pawiak. The German sitting on the driver's
right amused himself by beating pedestrians and Abram Traube
happened to be in reach of his thick cane and was hit on the
head. He fell, cracking his skull, cerebral inflammation fol-
lowed and death. He left a wife and four children . . . Basia's
husband, Herman, lost both parents in one week, they died of
typhus. Karol lost his mother, she died in custody. The old
lady had gone out for bread, she forgot to put on her armband,
she bumped into a police patrol who arrested her. She died of
a heart attack two weeks later. "Thank you, O God, that you
have preserved my dearest ones," sighs Jakub very quietly,
glancing tenderly at his wife, children, sons-in-law. He continues to read the *Hagadah*, trying to give his voice the usual
musical sound. The sobbing of women drowns him out. And
thus the sound of weeping is heard in every Jewish home that
evening. Concern for the future of one's nearest and dearest
chokes every heart with iron bands. Fathers close the *Hagadah*,
ending with the words, *Bshona haba b'jerushalaim* – Next year
in Jerusalem.'[15]

But if Passover was overshadowed by private fears, it was given more sinister overtones by a night of massacre which became known in the ghetto as the Night of Blood, or simply St Bartholomew's Eve. It happened on the very eve of Passover, but things had been boiling up for a few days, as Ringelblum reports:

'12 April 1942. Rumours are circulating that *Vernichtungs* (extermination) brigades have arrived in Warsaw . . . The hearsay talk is further fuelled because various foreign troops are based in Warsaw, Lithuanians, Ukrainians and so on who are waiting for an appropriate moment to organize a pogrom.'[16]

Marek Stok records:

'The Germans dragged 57 people from their homes and shot them in the streets close by their houses. The police cleared away the bodies next morning. They were carried away to the cemetery. Among those shot were a well-known baker, Blajman and his wife, there was some kind of printer, there was a teacher too, and a smuggler and so on. A very sombre mood prevails. Everyone is asking why precisely these people were taken out at night and killed . . . The Council sent around a reassuring circular: According to . . . the German authorities, the executions had a one-off character and will not be repeated.'[17]

But murder and blood lust continued unabated; however, an odd sort of comfort came from an unlikely source: the pockets of the German dead. Ringelblum writes:

'12 May 1942: They've brought 200,000 uniforms of dead soldiers to Warsaw. These uniforms were fearfully lice-ridden and sodden with blood. On the basis of the figure 200,000 in Warsaw alone you can imagine how many hundreds of thousands and millions fell in the East last winter. In the pockets of many uniforms . . . are letters from friends and families in the homeland (in Germany) which reflect the mood of the soldiers as well as that on the home front. The general impression is that the mood of the soldiers is rotten . . .'[18]

He adds another entry in similar vein:

'June 1942: It's interesting that the clothing is fearfully lice-ridden. As if the ghetto hadn't enough of its own lice, it has to get them from outside as well. Characteristically, in the pockets of murdered soldiers are often things they've plundered, including things from Warsaw, like, for example, haberdashery from Warsaw firms; even prayer shawls taken from the Jews now return to the Jews. There are more than 300,000 uniforms. So we can have our own ideas about the number of German soldiers who were killed last winter in frost-bound Russia.'[19]

Then, in July, at the solemn season of mourning for the destruction of the Temple, the head of the notorious killing squads, the *Einsatztruppen*, arrived in the ghetto.

Lawyer Marek Stok describes how shattered people were at this ominous news.

'On 18 or 19 July . . . we found young Kohn pale, shaken to the foundations, his nerves in shreds. He related the following to us and a few specially invited neighbours: the most dangerous, destructive team of the SS had arrived in Warsaw. This forecasts the complete destruction of all the Jews in Warsaw . . . The next day alarming rumours . . . circulated through the whole ghetto. The Council knew nothing officially. Just the same there was an enormous rush on all the workshops. Everybody tried to get enlisted in the workforce. For two or three days nothing else happened. Only the guard posts and walls were completely encircled by Latvians and SS as well as the Jewish Police. Suddenly, around 1 p.m. on the third day my wife ran into the factory with news that things were already bad on Chłodna Street and I shouldn't go back home. People were being killed one by one in their homes and on the street.

Everyone was gripped by total fear. That's what the Germans wanted, to terrorize people and make us totally disorientated ... notices about the 'deportations' have already appeared in the streets. We ran out to see these notices. They looked more or less like this: the Council announced that by command of the German authorities all the Jews living in the Jewish district of Warsaw would be deported to the East. Volunteers had to go to *Umschlagplatz* (the embarking point on Stawki Street where there was a railway siding) ... Here everyone would get 2 kg of bread and 1 kg of jam for the journey. Those who didn't go of their own free will would be taken by force. The deportation didn't involve: workers in German firms, workers in firms working for the army, Council workers, hospital workers, people involved in schools ... and so on ...'[20]

So the slaughter had begun – and one of the first victims of the 'Final Solution' was President Adam Czerniaków himself.

For days he had been desperately seeking information from one high ranking SS officer after another. His last diary entries run like this:

'18 July 1942: ... The day has been full of uneasy feelings. Rumours that deportations (of everyone?) will start from Monday evening. I asked the commissar if he knew anything about this. He told me, no, and that he didn't believe it would happen. At the same time there's a panic in the district, some people talk about deportations, others about a pogrom ...

'19 July 1942: Because of the panic I went round the whole area in a car ... I don't know if I managed to calm people. I did what I could, however. I try to raise the spirits of the delegations who come to see me. They don't know what it costs me. Today I took 2 headache powders. And cybalgine and valerian. In spite of that my head is bursting. I try to keep a smile stuck firmly to my lips.

'20 July 1942: At the Gestapo at 7.30 a.m. I asked Mende how much truth there was in the rumours. He answered that he has heard nothing. Next I made my way to Brandt, he said that he knew nothing . . . I felt very uncertain as I left his office. I turned to his boss, commissar Böhm. He replied that it's not his department . . . I mentioned that, according to all the news that's going about, the deportations have to start today at 7.30 p.m. He replied that if that were so he would certainly have known something about it. So, not having anywhere else to turn, I went to Scherer, the next in command in division III. He expressed surprise at these rumours and announced that he doesn't know anything either. In the end I asked if I might announce to the populace that there is no reason to fear. He replied that I may, that everything which they are talking about is *Quatsch und Unsinn* (stuff and nonsense).'[21]

The Gestapo bosses cynically led Czerniaków to believe that matters would be sorted out within the next couple of days. His entry for the next day, 22 July, however, shows that the rumours were only too true:

'Sturmbahnfuerer Höfle appeared at 10 a.m. with colleagues. We switched the telephones off. In the neighbouring garden the children were being taken away. They explained that – with certain exceptions – the Jews are to be deported to the East without any distinction of sex or age. 6,000 people must be ready to depart by 4 o'clock today. And at least that number every other day . . . Höfle (the officer for the deportation) ordered me into his office and told me that my wife is free for the moment, but if the deportations do not go according to plan she will be shot as first hostage.

'23 July 1942: In the Council. Worthoff of the resettlement division appeared. When I asked how many days in the week the ('resettlement') action would take place he said, seven days

45

in the week. In the town everyone is trying to open work-shops. A sewing machine may save a life.

'3 o'clock. 4,000 people are ready to depart. There's a clear order that there should be 9,000 by 4 o'clock.'[22]

Adam Czerniaków wrote no more entries in his diary. He penned a letter to his wife and another to his colleagues at the Jewish Council. Then he swallowed cyanide. He was found dead at his office desk. His letter to his wife said: 'They order me to murder the children of my people with my own hands. There's nothing left for me but to die.'[23]

To the Council he wrote:

'Worthoff and his colleagues were here and ordered me to get a children's transport ready for tomorrow. This has filled my bitter cup to the brim, for I cannot send defenceless children to death. I have decided to step aside. Don't regard this as an act of cowardice or a means of escape. I am powerless. My heart is breaking with sorrow and pity, I can't bear it any more. My action will show everyone the truth and perhaps set things back on the right path. I am aware that I am leaving you a difficult inheritance.'[24]

'Czerniaków's suicide – too late, a proof of weakness. He ought to have resisted. A weak man,' wrote Ringelblum testily in his *Chronicle*. And there were many in the ghetto who agreed. History, however, has taken a somewhat kinder view: Adam Czerniaków had been put in an impossible predicament, forced to sustain an unsustainable situation. He had made the enormous mistake of dealing with the Nazis – but he was faced with the need to save the lives of thousands. His death, however, did nothing to hold back the flood tide of murder which swept away the elderly and sick, young and old all through the hot summer days, the stifling nights of summer and early autumn 1942.

Notes

1 Quoted in *Text*.
2 Quoted in *Survive!*
3 *Chronicle*.
4 *Chronicle*.
5 *Letters*.
6 *Letters*.
7 *Letters*.
8 *Letters*.
9 *Letters*.
10 *Letters*.
11 *Letters*.
12 *Letters*.
13 *Letters*.
14 *Chronicle*.
15 *Memoirs*.
16 *Chronicle*.
17 *Memoirs*.
18 *Chronicle*.
19 *Chronicle*.
20 *Memoirs*.
21 *Diary*.
22 *Diary*.
23 Quoted in *Diary*.
24 Quoted in *Diary*.

CHAPTER 5

Deported to die

On 22 July 1942 the walls of the Warsaw ghetto were encircled by troops. These platoons, which included Ukrainian, Latvian and Lithuanian as well as German soldiers, drove people to *Umschlagplatz*, a sealed-off departure point, and thence into cattle trucks. The Jewish police had to hunt down their own people. One single poster in German and Polish announced the 'resettlement'. Many people deduced that those who were unable to work and a burden on the ghetto's slender resources would be the ones chosen to go 'further east'. The myth was that 'as long as we work we shall be safe' – but no one was safe from the cruel round-ups. A member of the Jewish Council wrote:

'They used the tactic of surprise, while at the same time they patrolled all the streets of the ghetto, sometimes entering all the houses simultaneously... They drove everyone ... downstairs at top speed and stood them in rows, to which new groups were added all the time; until finally the whole mass of people who had been collected were driven hastily to *Umschlagplatz*, where with equal haste they were loaded into the wagons ... Our total lack of knowledge about the course of the operation added to our fear, and so did the quiet which reigned around us, broken only by the constant echoes of pistol shots.'[1]

The first people to be deported were the destitute and the

refugees. The Jewish Police Officer, Jan Mawu*l*t, says the paupers were

'. . . indifferent about what would happen to them, they have already reached the bottom . . . The German and Czech Jews are quite different . . . They march in fours, regularly, in step like soldiers . . . Here comes a group of hospital patients . . . At the head is a doctor – a German Jew, with two sisters of mercy, all three wear, with pride which is reflected in their faces, distinguished war medals . . . 25 years ago they brought help to the wounded and dying . . . They came out whole from those battles; they passed through that fire. But they will not survive this battle. They will not come through this fire. Perhaps they sense this, but they hold themselves together proudly . . . The long cavalcades of people are headed for the north . . . for *Umschlagplatz*.

'The whole operation is called a blockade, a selection, an action, or campaign. The population recognizes these words quickly, they're on everybody's lips. "Where is the action today? Where are they blockading? Has the selection already finished on Gęsia Street?" These questions are being asked all the time.

'The population sees it all, but they don't believe their eyes, they can't understand . . . You hear gossip: "It won't last long, maybe they'll just take 40 or 50 thousand people, send them east – and that will be the end." . . . Yes, yes it's terrible, a frightful fate without any doubt, but what can we do? These people won't survive anyway; they drop dead every day . . . So if it's got to be this way perhaps they will be a ransom for us . . .

'The action is still going on . . . The whole thing is done at top speed, like lightning. Quick, quick, at a run! Now all the inhabitants are out in the yard, the selection's already been made, they've already separated the people who will return to their homes from those who will never see their homes again. They are not allowed to go slowly, although at a funeral you usually walk slowly, solemnly . . . Everybody who's been captured in the blockade is driven out to the road – several thousand people are grouped together in rows of four or six. Now the selection will take place. Row by row they approach the SS man. One glance at their documents, one at their face, a touch with the stick – to the left – to freedom, to the right – to *Umschlagplatz*. A group of privileged people is put apart on one side. They are the wives and children of the inner circle of the Jewish Police . . .

'Now there are three groups: the first, the privileged families of the functionaries, the second, workers who have been set free by the selection. They can go home. They are free. FOR THE MOMENT! The third group – that's the ones for *Umschlagplatz*. Thousands have been made to stand in fours, or rather, not stand but sit, for until the end of the selection all who must go to *Umschlagplatz* . . . must squat down in the road. Is this to be able to differentiate them more easily? Or so that no one might get away? Or simply a whim of the SS man. It's not clear. Now the selection is over . . . It's a hot August day, a heatwave, the women are in light summer dresses, in sandals, children are barefoot. No one has outer clothes, head-coverings . . . So have they to travel into the unknown like that? Impossible! Without a change of clothing, without any covers, without a piece of bread? . . . After all, they're going to the east, to Russia. What does this mean? What is happening here?

'There's no time to think . . . "Stand up! March!" They go. They go in an enormous procession, slowly, quickly – just as they are ordered. In front, behind and on all sides are Jewish Police Officers . . . Feverish talks . . . "Tell Mr X . . . I'm so-and-so's daughter, wife, mother. Get me out, sir! How much?"

These conversations go on the whole time; the people are hunted the whole time. Friends make a shield with their backs, block the Germans' line of vision . . . They save their relatives, their friends, their neighbours, they save for fun, for money. But the vast majority stay, they keep walking – and in the end they reach Umschlagplatz.'[2]

Once the first victims, the most wretched of the ghetto, had been driven away, the Jewish police started hunting down more people to fill the daily quotas. Tension and fear mounted unbearably. From the ghetto memoirs comes the following description by Stanislaw Sznapman.

'The blockades took place like this: the Germans assisted by Ukrainians and the Jewish Police surrounded a block of flats. The Jewish Police went through the house and summoned the people downstairs with their whistles, warning that those who stayed back would be shot. The Germans and Ukrainians simultaneously began to shoot and shout in order to increase fear and panic. People, ashen, shocked, sobbing and lamenting, went out to the street . . . People often went out in a state of undress, men in pyjamas, women in dressing gowns, the people who remained in the house, the elderly, children and the bedridden were killed . . . The spasmodic sobbing of women, the loud weeping of children mingled with the whistle and whack of the whips, falling on the faces and heads of the victims . . . It was a monstrous hell. In order to bring the bullying to its pitch and to torment the people to the extreme, still standing in rows, they were ordered to lie flat, stand and kneel for hours . . . Thus from 22 July from morning until evening the unfortunate victims of the barbarians were marched along the streets of the ghetto, beaten by batons and rifle butts, their faces turned to stone by pain, they were bowed under the weight of rucksacks and parcels, their last pieces of property:

'"And their bitter sobbing spreads abroad, Why, o, why, O Lord?"'[3]

On 6 August the murderers surrounded the ghetto orphanages and drove the children into the street. Janusz Korczak and Stefania Wilczyńska went to the death trains with their children. They are the most famous but they were not alone; other directors and assistants from children's homes and hospitals went too. The march of the children through the ghetto has become a legend, the subject of literature, drama and film.

Nachum Remba, Secretary to the Jewish Council, positioned himself at *Umschlagplatz* and did what he could to snatch people from the jaws of death. Ringelblum quotes Remba's description of the march of the children to the death trains on 6 August:

'That day completely finished me. A blockade of the "Small Ghetto" took place. They signalled to us that they're bringing in the nursing school, the pharmacists, Korczak's orphanage, the home on Śliska and Twarda Streets and many others. It was a roasting hot day. I put the children from the orphanages at the very edge of the square, under the walls. I judged that I might manage to protect them that afternoon, keep them until the next day. I suggested to Korczak that he come across to the Council with me to try to get some sort of intervention on his behalf. He refused, he didn't want to leave the children even for a minute, I stood beside the cordon of Jewish Police who were leading people to the wagons, I stood with a trembling heart as I watched to see if my plan would succeed. I kept asking how the quotas in each wagon were going. They kept on loading but there still wasn't a full complement. Suddenly Mr S ordered the orphanages to be put on board. I shall never forget that scene . . . In contrast to the milling crowds who went to the slaughter like cattle, a march was begun the like of which had never been before. All the children were put in fours, Korczak was at their head, his eyes turned upwards, he held two children by their little hands and led the procession. The second group was led by Stefania Wilczyńska, the third by Ms Broniatowska (her children had blue rucksacks), the fourth by Mr Szternfeld from the Home on Twarda. They were the first Jewish groups who went to death with dignity, casting looks at the barbarians which showed how much they despised them and how certain they were that they would be avenged for all the wrongs they had received. Even the Jewish police officers stood to attention and saluted. When the Germans saw Korczak they asked, 'Who is this man?' I couldn't hold out any longer, tears escaped from my eyes; I covered my face with my hands. Deep pain overcame me at the thought that we are so powerless, that I could do nothing, only stand by helplessly and watch the murder. At night it seemed to me that I could hear the tapping of children's little feet marching in time under the direction of their teachers. I heard the rhythmic, ceaseless patter of footsteps going off in an unknown direction . . .'[4]

Korczak and his children were transported from the ghetto on the Feast of the Transfiguration. The march of hundreds of children through the ghetto, their disappearance into the terrible dark wagons, underwent a transfiguration in people's memories: it was the slaughter of the innocents; and the horrific scene was touched by a sense of awe. The halo which shone about the little ones and their devoted teachers threw the appalling crime into an even darker shadow.

In a recently discovered piece of prose, Dr Korczak uses the whiteness of snow to transfigure, even sanctify the death of a child and his mother's silent grief. The short piece is set in Smocza Street, within the Warsaw ghetto.

'You know Smocza Street. It was always so. So many people

– they crowd together – they hurry – they quarrel and bargain – they shout out who has what to sell: this one has potatoes, this one cigarettes, this one a stock of clothing, this one sweets.

'And the pretty boy, quietly, very quietly, most quietly – was lying on the snow, was lying on white, lying on pure white snow.

'His mother was standing beside him, repeating again and again: "Please save him."

'Yes, it was certainly his mother . . . Only those words – and she didn't shout – she kept whispering clearly just this and nothing more: "Please save him."

'And people passed by, no one saved him – and they didn't do anything wrong, because he didn't need salvation.

'He is lying quietly and so serene, so bright on the white snow.

'His mouth is open a little as if he were smiling – I didn't notice what colour his lips were, but they were certainly pink. And his teeth were white.

'And his eyes are half-open, and in one eye, in the very centre – a small sparklet of light, probably a little star, the smallest of the small – a star shines.

'"Please save him, please save him."'[5]

'So bright on the white snow . . .' There was no snow that summer of slaughter in the Warsaw ghetto, but there was whiteness, a soft, shining falling not of snow but of feathers swirling in the golden light, feathers and down from ransacked homes shone in the brilliant sunlight of August and early September. Everything was covered with this light, undissolving 'snow'. A young freedom fighter in the Ghetto Uprising mentions the feathers in her book, *Farewell to 18, Miła Street.* Hela Rufeisen-Schupper describes the dangerous route the freedom fighters took through attics and lofts.

'The big attics in Polish homes which were used for drying linen were now secret roads. A white light shone here from the feathers and down which the Jews had poured out of their quilts and pillows in order to sell the casings ... for a piece of bread ... It was tough on the people walking across the attics because the feathers concealed the struts and it was difficult to jump from one strut to the other because you couldn't see them.'[6]

Although some adults might hide, the children were doomed. A young mother comments, 'Chance might decide the fate an adult, but as far as children were concerned – their fate had already been decreed. All the children were taken away.' Her account continues:

'A German with a really loutish-looking face and a whip in his hand was segregating out who had to stand on the left side and who on the right. The right side was a death sentence. No documents were checked. Sometimes the German asked about the work someone did, sometimes he simply looked at your face. I didn't have any certificates, any work cards and, over and above, I was holding my little son by the hand. All the women with children who were ahead of me had been directed to the right, which meant to *Umschlagplatz*. The German asked my husband about his job; he took a quick look at me. I hid my child under my coat, which I had lowered to the ground. I think the German noticed that manoeuvre. His whim of the moment saved our little threesome from death.'[7]

The world had gone mad. Normal patterns of human behaviour were overthrown. Parents in hiding murdered their children. Mothers with small children were denied access to hiding places. An eyewitness describes the following scene:

'A little fair-haired girl tore herself away from the kneeling group who had been condemned to die and fell back into the row (of five), like an arrow aimed straight from the skirts of her father's overcoat . . . But they chased her away. The infernal fear of collective responsibility. The whole fivesome might be taken because of her.'[8]

'In those days they said that "everyone has death in their eyes",' noted another memoir writer. 'We see skulls instead of faces.'[9]

'The threat of death was hanging over the whole ghetto,' adds Natan Żelichower. His memoir cries out with the ring of truth which underscores all these eyewitness reports.

'It was fearfully cramped and stuffy in the hiding place. We lay motionless so that we wouldn't betray our presence by the slightest rustle . . . We spent the days listening for echoes from the streets and yards – and these echoes were frequent and various. Every so often groups of the SS came into the yard together with Jewish Police and with fearful whistles summoned everyone out of the building . . . Our hearts froze with fear . . . as they were hunted down. Doors were torn off their hinges, windows and mirrors were broken; wardrobes were overthrown, filling the depths of the yard with fearful noise. And from time to time this symphony of destruction was cut through by the ear-piercing, dagger-sharp, heart-rending scream of a hunted victim. Then brutal German curses rang out and a series of shots finished it all.

'Once, when I was standing on guard beside a crack in the boards which closed the entrance to the loft I noticed a hand drawing aside the roofing paper . . . The head of an SS man appeared behind the hand. A deathly fear choked my throat, I gave a weak gesture to warn the others of the danger – and collapsed full length on top of the others in hiding who were lying on the floor . . . At the end of the following week I managed to . . . lodge myself and my family in a tiny room in the factory precincts . . . On 22 August I made my way to the factory floor. Suddenly shouts and running footsteps were heard. The gate I had just gone through was slammed shut. Cut off from the external world we waited for about two hours full of anxiety. When the gate was open the yard was now empty. The open doors frightened me. There was no one at home. I didn't want to believe the terrible truth . . . Blinded by the growing fear in me I ran towards the deportation square . . . I was out of my mind as I searched for my wife and daughter. A Jewish policeman from our factory floor stopped me. He started to say something but seeing that I didn't understand he pushed a little card into my hand. I read over and over again the words scribbled on the scrap of paper: "Dear Daddy. Save yourself. It seems that we are lost. I'm keeping mummy's spirits up as best I can. Perhaps fate will unite us again. Your Stella."

'It took a long time before I understood my daughter's last letter. I sat down on the kerb and wept bitterly . . . I was alone in the world – the most terrifying loneliness of all! For long hours I lay on my child's mattress, weeping into the pillow my longing for her . . .

'On Wednesday the manhunts started again. A gang of SS fell on the yard with yells of victory and whistles which put the whole house on alert. A moment later they started to run right through all the flats. The empty rooms reverberated with the manifold echoes of the Germans . . . The silence brought their voices to us with such clarity that we lost all sense of direction . . . We lived through the next hours with our nerves totally on edge. At 10 o'clock nine human beasts rushed into the yard, advertising their presence with shouts and shots. They ran all through the three hallways of our house and for half an hour we heard noises, shouts, laughter, oaths. But all was quiet with us. We barely breathed. A tall electrician stood above poor little Lilka with a quilt in his hand. Then the horde stormed back out to the yard again and left the house with drunken shouts. We were still quiet, only our breath came a little more easily. Lilka hadn't coughed – but would she last out next time?

'Twenty minutes went by – and suddenly Lilka began to cough – but the quilt landed on top of her and muffled the sound. From the landing we heard the joyful voice of a German: "Hans, komm. Hier sind Juden!" So the ninth man had been hiding in the gateway and waiting. Weakness riveted me to the spot. Footsteps ringing on the stairs cut through me like bullets from a gun . . . Then, in the fearful silence the cry of a baby resounded, full of unspoken accusation, a sorrowful, heart-rending wail. The footsteps stopped in front of the window. "A kid! Curse it," the German swore brutally. He tore the window open with a loud rasping sound. The infant, snatched from its covers, spiralled through the air and fell in a bloody pulp on the yard paving. The Germans went downstairs, stepped over their victim and headed for the gate. For an hour no one spoke a word. I looked dully at that bloody stain on the road and in my brain I felt emptiness, not even horror any more – not despair – not a longing to live or fight, only a terrible emptiness which slowly changed to an enormous sorrow inside me . . .'[10]

When the 'action' ended the survivors slipped away, 'creeping close to the walls of the houses'. A child's cough had nearly given them away. An abandoned baby's forlorn wail had saved their lives. And now as I walk over the area where the ghetto once stood I buy vegetables, meat and bread, but the child's wail is still in my thoughts. I remember the words of a Polish friend. Too young to remember the war personally, she recalls that her father had said, 'Don't go there, where the ghetto stood: it is a place of blood, a place of death.' But thousands come now, from all over the world with flowers and candles, with stones and prayers, with thoughts of remembrance. And this is right. We need to hear that child's cry; it was, all unwitting, both victim and saviour. The footsteps of a thousand children walking to their deaths must never be forgotten. Many, like Stella, went bravely, comforting the little ones, consoling their distressed relatives. Her letter to her father gave him courage to live. Because she had said, 'Perhaps fate will unite us again', her father decided not to die. He survived concentration camps and returned to Warsaw at the end of the war and his memoir ends: 'I stood on the ruins of the Warsaw ghetto; there is no trace of houses or streets. It is a field of dumb bricks and ruins; a monstrous illustration of the right to survive which I have described.'[11]

The ruins have been rebuilt, but the words remain to show us how it was; and in them are the tears, the suffering and the heroism of branded Jewish children. There was no quietness or beauty in their deaths but as we remember them perhaps their tears will turn to laughter in the golden light of summer, their sleep be gentle in the 'pure white' of winter snow – and their torments will turn to angel feathers to soothe the sorrow of children who suffer.

Notes

1 *Memoirs.*
2 *Memoirs.*
3 *Memoirs.*
4 *Chronicle.*
5 Quoted in *Text.*
6 Hela Rufeisen-Schupper, *Farewell to 18, Miła Street* (*Pożegnanie Miłej 18*), Beseder, Krakow, 1996. The author, who kindly gave me permission to use this extract from her personal story, asked me to note that the first edition of her book appeared in 1990

in Israel. A German translation has been published by SKRIBA
Verlag.

7 *Memoirs.*
8 Quoted in *Survive!*
9 *Memoirs.*
10 *Memoirs.*
11 *Memoirs.*

CHAPTER 6

Umschlagplatz:
Place of departure, descent into hell

Umschlagplatz, the enclosed ground where people were held before they were deported to the death camp of Treblinka, is commemorated by a stark marble memorial shaped like one of the cattle wagons into which hundreds of people were crammed. The outer wall is bordered with a single black stripe, reminiscent of the tallith, or prayer shawl. On it is engraved the name, *Umschlagplatz*. Above the entrance a black plaque depicts a forest of fallen trees, and the wall opposite has an opening which looks out on to a growing tree, a sign of life, continuity, hope – and a reminder that just such a small opening led hundreds of thousands to their deaths. Words are carved on the internal walls: 350 Jewish names, symbolically chosen, the names of the dead. A plaque in English, Hebrew, Polish and Yiddish says, 'Along this path of suffering and death over 300,000 Jews were driven from the Warsaw ghetto to the gas chambers of the Nazi extermination camps, 1942–43.' There are also words from the Book of Job: 'O earth, do not hide my blood, so that my cry will never end' (Job 16.18).

Pope John Paul's tour of Poland in June 1999 included a visit to the Jewish memorial, at which Dr Marek Edelman, the only survivor of the Command of the Jewish Fighting Force, conversed with his compatriot in front of the cameras of the world. Their words were not audible, but the 20 million viewers in Poland who tuned in to the Papal tour would have seen Dr Edelman pointing with his hand this way and that, explaining the events which will be recorded in this chapter. It is good that there was no sound, for the *Umschlagplatz* is truly a place of memory. Heavy traffic roars by on the main road outside, but within the monument there is stillness.

Marek Edelman's report, written in 1946, *The Ghetto is Fighting*, describes *Umschlagplatz*:

'High walls surround it, heavily guarded by Jewish Police, broken only in one very narrow place. It is to this very entrance that groups of hopeless, powerless people are led. They are all holding papers of some sort or another, work cards, identity cards. The guard at the entrance casts a quick glance at them. 'Right' – that means life. 'Left' means death. Although we already know that persuasion doesn't help, each person tries to show how essential they are for German production, for the German boss and pleads for the little word, 'Right'. But the sentry doesn't even listen. Sometimes he chooses short people – right! Another time he excludes blonde women and girls – left. In the morning he picks out small people, in the evening he favours tall ones. Left, left, left. The wave of people swells, deepens, floods over the whole square, the large three-storey buildings of the school. There are more people than are needed for even a four-day quota. People are 'in reserve'. They have been waiting for four or five days to be loaded into the wagons. People fill every empty space, crowd into the buildings, camp out in empty class rooms, corridors, stairs. Dirty, slimy mud pours over the floors. There's no water in the taps, the toilets are blocked. At every step you sink into excrement. The smell of sweat and urine is stifling. The nights are cold, there's no glass in the windows. Some people are only wearing night-clothes, dressing gowns ... Children, fevered, sweating, lie listlessly in their mothers' arms. Adults shrink into themselves, become small, grow grey. All faces have one single expression. Wild, mad fear, pale, powerless despair, a sudden revelation that the worst thing, the incredible thing, the thing which right to the last moment no one wanted to believe, is inevitably bound to happen ... An old man clings feverishly, beseechingly to the strangers who are beside him. A mother cuddles her three children to her in powerless torment. You want to shout – but there's no one to listen, you want to argue, to beg, but there's no one, you are alone, utterly alone in this crowd of thousands; and tens, no, thousands of guns are aimed at your heart, the Ukrainian guards grow before your very eyes until they are as big as giants, and now you don't know anything, you don't think about anything, you sit dully in the corner in the mud and filth of the wet floor. And round about you it gets more stifling, more overcrowded, not at all because of all those bodies pressed close together, not from the stench and stuffiness of the rooms, but from a sudden feeling that everything is lost, that there's nothing more to be done any more, that now you've got to die.'[1]

Marek Edelman's duties as a hospital orderly took him freely to the Polish side and he had every opportunity to hide there, but he refused. In the hot summer days of 1942 he worked at *Umschlagplatz* and witnessed the scenes he recorded in his report. Dr Edelman survived the war to become a distinguished cardiologist. In 1998 he was awarded the White Eagle, Poland's highest award.

Another writer, Stefania Staszewska, was 14 when she and her mother were taken to *Umschlagplatz* – to be parted for ever:

'Our square looked like an enormous bazaar with thousands of people circling from place to place, where hundreds of children whose faces were swollen with weeping searched in vain for their parents. It was a fearful fairground where money had no worth, while fortune and chance, on the other hand, decided one's fate . . . To make their "work" easier the Germans ordered everyone to kneel down or squat . . . Machine gun butts struck the heads of the dilatory. The Germans . . . tore boards from the fence and hit out at any heads which were raised from the ground. Crouching, we awaited the end of this show. My hair was stuck to my forehead, I wiped my eyes with blackened hands, my clothing was dirty and torn from crawling across the stones, I was wild with thirst, I had dust in my teeth – and a stone in my heart. Yes, a stone, because I felt nothing at that moment except an animal desire to live, and fear of death, of gas. With dry eyes I looked at heads pouring with blood, at young girls who were sent to death, at the parting of families, at children being torn from their mothers and at the sacrifice of mothers who chose to die with their children. With indifferent eyes I looked at the weeping victims of sadistic Germans who at this time fraught with danger tried to flirt with girls or threaten children. At this moment I thought only about Mum and myself. A miracle was needed to get out of this death-trap . . .

'Crawling on all fours we approached the gate. There were perhaps 500 people ahead of us. Suddenly Mum touched my hand. "Listen to me, child, if the Germans set you free but send me to the wagons, remember you are not to come with me, you are young, you must live, I am old, I'm 40 and I'm ill, but you must live." O, Mother, Mother . . . in spite of the certainty that I had heard those words from you, I still have the awful feeling that it was me who left you, that I made use of your permission to leave. O God! O God! My conscience will never be clean now, I feel that this was the hour of my death, the death of my "me", of my heart, of my real life . . . Yes, Mother, I should have perished with you then . . . We came nearer and nearer to the place of control. A cart loaded with cases and bags stopped in front of us . . . Suddenly one of the Ukrainians fired his gun right beside the cart, the horses reared on their hind legs . . . Panic ensued, several cases fell off the cart, one fell on my head and when I had dug myself out almost from under the cart and raised myself to my knees Mum was no longer beside me. I stood on the case. I shouted, "Mum!" but she had disappeared somewhere and unfortunately I could no longer see her. Just at that moment a Ukrainian roared in my ear, "*sadi!*" (sit down!) and made to hit me with a board. I knelt down not knowing what to do . . . Suddenly some German pointed at me, "Du, Mädchen". He ordered me to get up and go to the control. I stood at the end of a small queue . . . I longed to hear the word "*rechts*". I longed to stay alive, to live, to live. I didn't have much chance, I was little, in tears, dirty with a huge pack on my back. But now it's my turn. My legs tremble with fear. I stretch out my hand with my identity card, my heart thumped as if it were a hammer, my eyes were fixed on the mouth of the judge. I gaze into his eyes; now I feel certain that my eyes can extract the word "life" from his lips . . . Slowly he raises his hand, his left hand. I died with fear: so it's to be "left" after all? I looked him in the eyes, he looked at me and his hand abruptly switched to the right. The Jewish policeman shoved me through the gate on to Zamenhof Street.

'I had survived. I'm alive. My heart pounds, my legs shake. I ran a few steps forward but suddenly my happiness deserted me. What about Mother? O, my dear Mother, can anyone understand the pain and conflict which tore my soul just then?

I'm rejoicing because I'm alive, but my poor Mum is there, alone, deserted. I stood still in the road and then I ran first to one side, then to the other like a mad thing. Something pushed me forward, and something held me back. No, no, I mustn't go back, because death is there. And again the internal struggle. Mum, Mum is there too. I burst into tears; I sobbed, standing in the empty street.'[2]

Some people were snatched away to safety by members of the underground, by hospital workers, even by the Jewish Police who guarded the route from *Umschlagplatz* to the death trains. Published in English as *The Pianist*, Władysław Szpilman's remarkable account describes his rescue as he and his family made their way out to the train.

'The train came into sight: more than a dozen cattle trucks and goods trucks rolling slowly towards us. The evening breeze, blowing in the same direction, wafted a suffocating wave of chlorine our way . . . We got ready to leave. Why wait? The sooner we were in the trucks the better. A line of police was stationed a few paces from the train, leaving a broad path open for the crowd. The path led to the open doors of the chlorinated trucks . . . the smell of chlorine made breathing difficult, even some distance from the trucks. What went on in there if the floors had to be so heavily chlorinated? We had gone about halfway down the train when I suddenly heard someone shout, "Here! Here, Szpilman!" A hand grabbed me by the collar, and I was flung back and out of the police cordon . . .

'I shouted like someone possessed . . . One of the policemen turned and looked angrily at me.

'"What the hell do you think you're doing? Go on, save yourself!"

'Save myself? From what? In a flash I realized what awaited the people in the cattle trucks. My hair stood on end. I glanced behind me. I saw the open compound, the railway lines and platforms, and beyond them the streets. Driven by compulsive animal fear, I ran for the streets, slipped in among a column of Council workers just leaving the place, and got through the gate that way.

'When I could think straight again, I was on a pavement among buildings. An SS man came out of one of the houses with a ˥ policeman. The SS man had an impassive, arrogant ceman was positively crawling to him, smiling, lance. He pointed to the train . . . and said . . . go for meltdown!"

way he was pointing. The doors of the trucks ', and the train was starting off, slowly and ned away and staggered down the empty t loud, pursued by the fading cries of the hose trucks. It sounded like the twittering dly peril.'[3]

ssible to escape from *Umschlagplatz* and

d
ev
Wł
your,
next (
and ad

'Ofte
taking p(
himself, (
our brave
had been s

An extra(
how hospita

'There we
hospital units

:ky enough to be snatched away, like he chances were that you would find milling crowds of doomed people the cites one or two successful escapes,

the person who is supposed to be doesn't succeed . . . but falls victim wagons with the crowd. One of ostrzynski, perished like this, he collect one of our comrades.'[4]

an unknown woman describes ople escape:

nurses or people working in al free access to the Square

carried somebody out disguised as a nurse or a hospital worker. Small children were sometimes carried out in rucksacks, having been previously drugged so that they wouldn't betray their presence as they passed by Germans. There were cases, though more rarely, of taking people who were alive out by funeral cart. The living person was put under the corpses and carted out of the Square. Everyone saved themselves as best they could.'[5]

The young people of the Jewish resistance had been trying to rouse people's awareness of the Nazis' extermination plans from the very beginning of the 'deportation action'. Marek Edelman records how the periodical produced by the Bund, *Off der Wach* (On Guard), urged people to resist. 'Don't let yourselves be caught, fight with your hands, your feet.'[6]

To back up their warnings, the Bund sent one of its members, Zalmen Frydrych, also known as Zygmunt, out to follow the route of the Jewish deportees. Marek Edelman reports:

'His journey "to the east" took no time at all, barely three days. As soon as he had got through the ghetto wall he got into contact with railway workers at Gdańsk Station working on the Warsaw–Malkinia line and travelled off with them in the wake of the transport. He got as far as Sokolów where, as local railway men informed him, the railway line split in two and a siding went off in the direction of Treblinka. Every day a Warsaw goods train goes along that line full of people and returns empty. There is no extra transport of provisions. Civilians are forbidden to enter the station at Treblinka. This is irrefutable evidence that the people transported there are killed. The next day Zygmunt met two naked Jews in Sokolów market, fugitives from Treblinka. They described the executions exactly. So it wasn't something someone had thought up but the facts were confirmed by eyewitnesses (one of the fugitives was our comrade Wallach).

After Zygmunt had got back a second number of *Oif der Wach* was printed in which we gave an exact description of Treblinka. But even so the Jews stubbornly refused to believe.'[7]

The truth was so unspeakable that grief-stricken people left behind in the reduced ghetto area in Warsaw simply couldn't take it in. Wild rumours circulated. They had been used to seeing vast numbers of people from all over Europe deported to Warsaw; they now claimed to have received postcards from friends who had been forced to leave saying they had arrived safely, that they were working in the fields, that there was enough to eat. When pressed for further details people would admit that they hadn't actually read the postcards themselves, but a friend of a friend had . . .

Emanuel Ringelblum, whose *Chronicle* pauses in shock and horror as 'the flood of resettlement carries everything away', notes:

'Three hundred thousand Jews from Warsaw have been murdered in the death camp in Treblinka, but . . . people's fantasy can't accept this fearful thought and looks for various ways of deluding oneself and others . . . They couldn't understand that it's possible to murder tens of thousands of innocent women, children, men outright in this way . . . when it was recognized that it's totally impossible, then you still have to reply: where have more than 300,000 Warsaw Jews got to? Where have 300,000 Polish Jews perished? And the answer was found. People began to weave legends about letters from deportees from definite areas: Brest, Kowel, Pińsk and so on. No matter how hard you try, you never manage to get to the person who had read such a letter. It was always some third person who had heard from someone else that some Mr X or Y had read this letter . . .

'I am firmly convinced that even today, when the remaining

handful of Warsaw Jews knows very well what Treblinka is, a few hundreds, and perhaps thousands, of people will still believe the false news about the supposed children's camps . . . A few days ago a rumour went round that 2,000 children had returned from Treblinka. I believe that many years after the war, long after all the secrets of the death camps have been revealed, unhappy mothers will still dream that the children who were torn from them are somewhere far away in Russia. They will organize expeditions to search for thousand-fold masses of starving Jews.'[8]

Ringelblum also reports that people began to ask the unanswerable question: why?

'Why? Why was there no opposition when the deportation of 300,000 Jews from Warsaw began? Why did they allow themselves to be led like sheep to the slaughter? Why did the enemy manage to do it so easily, so smoothly? Why did the perpetrators not sustain even one loss? Why could 50 SS men (others say even fewer), with the help of a division of about 200 Ukrainians and as many Latvians, accomplish it so smoothly?'[9]

There was another burning question. Why had the Jewish Police turned on their own people and acted as slavish servants of the Gestapo? Some men had defiantly thrown aside their badge of office, their baton and belt and had refused to take part in the 'action'; but most, believing that they could still protect themselves or their families, were driven to terrible cruelties as they hunted out a new quota of 'heads' each day for *Umschlagplatz*.

Ringelblum addresses the problem:

'There remains the eternal puzzle of the passivity of the Jewish people also against their police. At this present moment, now that people have already cooled off a little and are taking stock of what has happened, the feeling of shame is growing that no one resisted even our own police.

Umschlagplatz: *Place of departure, descent into hell*

'They recall who bears the guilt of mass murder and come to the conviction that the Jewish Police are very guilty. Some people even say that the only culprits are the Jewish Police. And now people take revenge. At every opportunity they remind the police of their guilt. Every policeman I've spoken to claims total innocence. He never took part in an action . . . in the best case he actually saved people; others captured them, but not he . . .

'People tell all sorts of fearful stories about the behaviour of the Jewish Police at *Umschlagplatz*. People weren't people for them any more but "heads" from whom they could get bribes . . . money, diamonds, gold etc . . . They didn't know what compassion is . . . People at *Umschlag*, especially women, put up a fight. That all created an unbearable atmosphere for the police who went mad like savages and committed frightful crimes.'[10]

As a footnote to the tragedy of the Jewish Police, Ringelblum records the final deception when the main deportations were over, the ghetto had been turned into a concentration camp and the Gestapo had no more need of the police:

'They collected several hundred men on Szczęśliwa Street. A supposed blockade was said to be about to be carried out there – with their help – on 16 September. Meantime the Ukrainians and SS went to the block on Ostrowska Street which is where the police lived, and ordered the women and children to come out as if they were to be registered. They . . . sent them all – about 800 women and children – to *Umschlagplatz* and loaded them into the wagons. Their husbands learnt about the misfortune during the fake blockade. They ran to *Umschlagplatz* but once they were there the SS warned them they would shoot everyone who approached the wagons. Nobody moved from their place, weeping they all bade farewell to their deported wives.'[11]

In the wake of the deportations a new mood affected the enslaved workforce of the ghetto: a desire for revenge. Young people of the Jewish underground longed for weapons. On the 'other' side of the wall the Polish underground press published news of the horror. A group of Catholic intellectuals who had formed a movement called the Front for the Rebirth of Poland published 5,000 copies of a special pamphlet entitled *Protest*. Its author was a well-known writer, Zofia Kossak-Szczuka:

'In the Warsaw ghetto, behind the wall separating them off from the world, several hundreds of thousands of condemned people are waiting for death. No hope of rescue exists for them, no help is to be found anywhere . . . The world looks at this crime which is more terrible than anything we have ever seen – and is silent . . . The Jews are dying surrounded only by Pilate who washes his hands.

'This silence can be tolerated no longer . . . It is not permissible to remain passive in the face of crime. The person who is silent in the face of murder becomes an accomplice of the murderer. If we do not condemn – we consent.

'And so we, Catholic Poles, raise our voices . . . We do not want to be Pilate. The blood of the defenceless cries for vengeance to heaven . . .'[12]

Shocked at the continuing massacre, some people tried to help their doomed friends and the movement known as *Żegota* was formed by Zofia Kossak – its explicit aim was to give aid to Jews.

The Jews in the ghetto were convinced that if the world at large – and the leaders of the Allied Powers in particular – knew of their fate they would receive rescue and relief on a large scale. Accordingly, one August evening in 1942 two Jewish leaders met with a Polish resistance worker, an important go-between who linked the Home Army in Warsaw with the

Polish government in London. His name in the underground was Jan Karski. He would take out first-hand accounts of the mass murder of Polish Jews – but the leaders of the world would remain silent.

Notes

1 *The Ghetto is Fighting.*
2 *Memoirs.*
3 W. Szpilman, *The Pianist*, Gollancz, London, 1999.
4 *Ghetto.*
5 *Memoirs.*
6 *Ghetto.*
7 *Ghetto.*
8 *Chronicle.*
9 *Chronicle.*
10 *Chronicle.*
11 *Chronicle.*
12 *Protest*, quoted in *Polish Help for Jews*, an exhibition in the Pawiak Museum, Warsaw in 1999.

CHAPTER 7

Freedom fighters defend
the ghetto

Minor acts of resistance were carried out during the 'resettle-ment'. For example, forced labour gangs who had to sort through possessions of those who had been murdered, sabotaged Jewish property so that it wouldn't fall into Nazi hands. Natan Żelichower records his experience:

'This new work completely paralysed my movements. For suddenly I found myself in homes of people I had known . . . in homes where we came upon a table set for breakfast or dinner, with pots full of food in the kitchen; in homes which had not yet lost the smell of life . . . These flats were still alive . . . We broke up doors, smashed mirrors, destroyed French polish; we were careless as we took down lamps, breaking them into small pieces as we lowered them to the floor. We trans-formed curtains into strips of rag and poured ink over sofas.'[1]

There was religious resistance too. Historian Emanuel Ringelblum (whose life and work within the ghetto was con-tinuous active resistance) described how at *Umschlagplatz*, 'The well-known writer and journalist Hillel Zeitlin . . . clothed himself in a tallith and liturgical funereal robes.' Ringelblum also notes the example of Rabbi Nutkiewicz:

'He went hungry and endured cold, sacrificing his strength for the common good. During the "deportations" he was caught at *Umschlagplatz*. Realizing without a shadow of doubt what awaited him at Treblinka, he resisted the criminals. He jumped down from the wagon into which he had been pushed. A Ukrainian in the convoy shouted at him to get back in or he would be shot. Rabbi Nutkiewicz replied decisively, "Shoot! I'm not getting in.""[2]

In this action, which cost his life, Rabbi Nutkiewicz anticipated the opposition which would be put up by the young freedom fighters of the ghetto who declared: 'No one will go to the wagons!'

Boys and girls in organized youth movements had been active from the very beginning. While many people felt isolated even in conditions of extreme overcrowding, the youth organizations offered their members a sense of belonging, a wider vision and a network of mutual support which extended beyond the ghetto. After the war Cywia Lubetkin, who with her husband Yitzhak Zuckerman had been a major figure in the ghetto resistance, wrote:

'. . . our fate would have turned out differently if we had not been part of a Movement and if from early childhood we had not assimilated the values it had taught us . . . It was only thanks to the education we had been given that we were able to survive that dreadful time.'[3]

During the massacres of summer 1942 young people had ached to defend their doomed and persecuted people. But they had no weapons and they were impeded by the fear of 'collective responsibility' – and by their more cautious elders who warned them: 'We cannot save those who have been condemned to death but armed reaction on our part might threaten the lives of the thousands who remain.' The more religious said that one should not resist the will of the Eternal God. 'The Lord gives, the Lord takes away. Blessed be the Name of the Lord.'[4]

Nevertheless, on 28 July 1942, just six days after the start of the 'deportation', members of three youth movements, Ha-Shomer ha-Za'ir, Dror He-Halutz and Akiva, met at the Dror kibbutz at 34 Dzielna Street and formed the Jewish Fighting Force, which became known by its Polish initials ŻOB.

The newly formed fighting force went into action at once. They posted notices up all over the ghetto: 'Don't go to Treblinka. Don't trust your work cards. Hide your little ones and old people. Young people, defend yourselves however you can. Better to die from a bullet in the ghetto than to be exterminated in Treblinka!'

ŻOB despatched couriers to get hold of weapons, to stir up resistance in other ghettos. Twenty-eight-year-old Fruma (or Frumka) Plotnicka, whose heroism had been applauded by Emanuel Ringelblum, was sent out to the Polish side of the wall to procure weapons and smuggle them into the ghetto. With her went Arie Wilner who, like Fruma, was already a seasoned veteran. Also known by the Polish name Jurek, 24-year-old Arie had been a Ha-Shomer kibbutz leader in the ghetto and had links with the Polish Scouting movement. In spite of strict controls at the ghetto gates Fruma and Arie returned successfully to base with hand grenades hidden in a bag of potatoes; and the young people undertook their first acts of armed resistance. On 20 August they carried out an attempted execution of the most hated man in the ghetto: Jozef Szeryński, the chief of the Jewish Police. Twenty-one-year-old Izrael Kanal was detailed for the job. A member of the youth movement Akiva, Izrael had joined the Jewish Police on the orders of his organization. His inside knowledge made him an obvious candidate for the job. He put on his policeman's cap and rang the bell of the chief's private flat. When Szeryński came out, Izrael shot him. The bullet did not kill, but although the attempt had failed the psychological breakthrough was all-important. There was joy in the ŻOB headquarters that night. With their own money they purchased more weapons, revolvers and hand grenades which were smuggled into the ghetto.

But then things fell apart. ŻOB had sent 70 young people out to the forests to join forces with Polish Communist partisans. But the Poles had barely started to organize underground resistance and life for Jews beyond the walls of the ghetto was so dangerous that very few survived. Then on 3 September ŻOB suffered a crushing blow when one of its leaders, Jozef Kaplan, was arrested by the Gestapo. Another key member, Shmuel Breslaw, tried to rescue his comrade but was shot by a German bullet.

ŻOB now decided to move its store of arms to another hiding place and a young girl, Regina Justman, was given the task of carrying the revolvers and grenades in a bag of vegetables. Unfortunately she was searched, the weapons were confiscated and Regina lost her life.

'Only three members of the leadership remained,' wrote Cywia Lubetkin. 'Izrael Kanal, Yitzhak Zuckerman and me. Great spiritual strength was required to begin again.'[5]

At this point, however, 23-year-old Mordecai Anielewicz, a youth leader of Ha-Shomer ha-Za'ir, returned to the ghetto. 'A talented lad, well-read, full of energy,' is how Dr Marek Edelman described him many years after the war. 'Expansive, full of enthusiasm.'[6]

Emanuel Ringelblum writes:

'I became acquainted with this young man at the start of the war. Of medium height, with a narrow, pale, pointed face, long hair and a pleasant exterior, he was dressed in sports clothes when he came to borrow a book. After that he often came to borrow books on Jewish history, and on economics, in which he was very interested. Who could guess that this quiet, modest, nice young boy would, three years later, become the most significant man in the ghetto whose name some people would pronounce with honour, others – with fear?'[7]

As well as being involved in the ghetto archives, Mordecai Anielewicz was co-editor of an underground bulletin which gave daily reports of radio broadcasts from London and Moscow. He was a leader of the Ha-Shomer commune at 24 Nalewki Street. Dr Ringelblum's recollections continue, primly:

'The war demoralized Jewish young people terribly. Their one ideal was a riotous life. Cards, vodka, women, narrow egoism became the plague of Jewish youth, the great majority of whom lost all interest in any form of social work ... Ha-Shomer ha-Za'ir, under the leadership of comrade Mordecai, was one of the cells to which young people with ideological commitment came, in whom the spark of idealism had not been extinguished, together with a readiness to sacrifice oneself for the common good ... Mordecai was unusually dedicated to his comrades in a way which is rarely met in organizations or parties. He was ready to leap into the fire for their sakes ...'[8]

So Mordecai had already won respect within the ghetto. He took over the command of the Jewish Fighting Force and the young people started to prepare for armed action. Links with the Polish Home Army (Armia Krajowa, or A.K.) came through Scouting contacts. But as far as active support and supplies of weapons went, the response remained disappointing. The Home Army, suspicious of the young freedom fighters with their left-wing, Communist sympathies, refused to see them as an official body in the ghetto. The young people accordingly reconsolidated themselves as a Jewish National Committee, with the Fighting Force as a wing.

By the end of October negotiations with other Jewish underground groups were successfully carried through and the Bund now joined the Jewish Fighting Force in the Warsaw ghetto. Marek Edelman explains:

'We decide to form a common fighting organization with the aim of putting up armed resistance to the Germans in the event of a repetition of an extermination action. We understand that only coordinated work and the highest common effort will give any kind of result.'[9]

The core leadership of ŻOB consisted of five young people. Marek Edelman gives their joint ages as 110. Other resistance movements besides ŻOB were the Jewish Military Union and two religious groups, Mizrachi and Agudat Yisrael, but the Jewish Fighting Force was the main focus of the Uprising. Their first armed act was to carry out two executions on men the ghetto viewed as traitors: Jakob Lejkin, the Deputy Commander of the Jewish Police, and Izrael First, the director of the compromised Jewish Council. ŻOB posted notices throughout the ghetto explaining who had carried out the death sentences and why. They publicly convicted managers of Jewish slave labour and members of the Jewish Council who had collaborated with the enemy. The aim was to cleanse the ghetto of corruption so that people would be united in resistance. Yet still there was an almost total lack of weapons and ŻOB was in a state of constant tension in case more deportations began before the young fighters could arm themselves in any significant way.

And indeed, the next German 'action' in January 1943 took the ŻOB leadership by surprise, because it came at a time when the Germans were harrying Poles so that, ironically, the ghetto seemed a relatively safe place. So everyone was startled when they woke up on the morning of 18 January to find that the ghetto gates were heavily guarded and another liquidation action was about to begin. 'This time, however,' Marek Edelman reports, 'the Germans didn't succeed in carrying out their plans with impunity.'[10]

Cywia Lubetkin describes how she and other young people had spent the entire night before the unexpected attack listening to 'a dear guest', the poet Yitzhak Katzenelson, who had just lost his wife and two small children, read his latest work:

'We had hardly fallen asleep when a sentry ran up and informed us that troop movements have been noted . . . We saw that all the streets have been surrounded and a German guard is posted at every block. There's no way we could get out to the street . . . All our groups were isolated. Every unit, depending on its store of weapons, had to depend entirely on itself.'[11]

Although they had been taken by surprise the freedom fighters went into action. The first shots were fired by Arie Wilner when the Germans began to hunt through homes of ŻOB members. Mordecai Anielewicz led his fighters into the ranks of people who were being led away to *Umschlagplatz* and Treblinka. They kept their pistols and hand grenades hidden until Mordecai ordered them to fire. And now ŻOB had, as Marek Edelman reports, 'its baptism by fire. We lost the flower of our organization there.' The young people found themselves fighting with pistols face to face with well-trained, massively armed soldiers. There were some German casualties, but most of the fighters fell. Cywia Lubetkin writes:

'Out of the whole group only Mordecai Anielewicz and a girl survived. When his ammunition ran out Mordecai tore a rifle from one of the Germans, withdrew to a doorway and went on shooting from there. The Germans were afraid to go into the house. Some Jews were in hiding not far away. One of them jumped out and pulled Mordecai Anielewicz into their midst. The Germans set fire to the house.'[12]

Freedom fighters defend the ghetto

All over the ghetto people had gone into hiding wherever they could. No one now trusted in work permits to save them; shouts of 'Juden 'raus' brought no one into the streets. The Germans therefore had to enter every house and search for their victims. 'So we decided not to go out and attack them on the street, but to wait for the enemy to come to us. We supposed that the Germans wouldn't be over-cautious since they didn't know we were waiting for them with weapons in our hands,' writes Cywia Lubetkin, describing a set-to in a house where groups of young fighters were positioned under the command of Yitzhak Zuckerman.[13]

'After so many frightful years we did not imagine that when we began to open fire on the Germans and kill them we would come out alive. We took up our positions, 40 boys and girls under the leadership of Yitzhak Zuckerman. We had four hand grenades and four revolvers. The majority were armed with iron rods, sticks and weapons we'd made ourselves – bottles filled with vitriol . . . We waited in suspense for the Germans to arrive and told ourselves: the hour of vengeance is coming. If we must die, we shall perish with a quiet conscience . . .

'The clatter of nailed boots was heard on the stairs. Doors were flung open and a group of Germans pushed into the room. The first people they met were Zecharia Artstein and Hanoch Gutman . . . Zecharia was sitting in the corridor, apparently reading, so they didn't pay any attention to him. We were all scattered throughout the neighbouring rooms, hiding behind cupboards. The Germans didn't stop but went through the first room and entered ours. They saw a few people – pathetic young Jews who were apathetically awaiting their executioners. At that moment Zecharia leapt from his place, shot the Germans in the back and killed two. The remainder, shocked, retreated to the stairs. The comrades who had been hiding in the rooms threw themselves after them. Meir Finkelstein, who was first, was hit and got a German bullet in his mouth. Hanoch Gutman was standing behind him. He managed to jump out through the narrow entrance and wound the fleeing German at the end . . . Zecharia and Hanoch collected weapons from the dead and wounded Germans. The others chased the escapees.

'For a few moments we were happy. We had seen with our own eyes Germans fleeing in panic. Soldiers who had beaten the world were fleeing from a Jewish kid armed with only a pistol or hand grenade . . .'[14]

The skirmishes lasted for four days and the moral victory was real, even though there were heavy losses. But while, in the summer round-ups, five or six thousand people had been crammed into the death trains every day, now in January, as a result of the resistance offered by the young fighters it took four days for the Germans to gather that number – many of whom were the sick and elderly – and they required about 200 German guards and 800 Ukrainian, Latvian and Lithuanian troops to carry out the task. On the last day of the 'action' a massive slaughter was carried out – probably as an act of revenge – and about a thousand people perished beneath a storm of bullets.

Although ŻOB had sustained heavy losses the January campaign marked a turning point for the Jews in the ghetto and for the Poles on the other side of the wall. The young people had shown that the Jews were no longer passive victims but a force to be reckoned with – and the SS were not invincible. Resistance was possible.

People now clamoured to join the Fighting Force, whose young leaders became the controlling power in the ghetto, totally supplanting the redundant and compromised Jewish

Council. To procure arms the ŻOB leadership taxed the well-to-do. They limited their own rations to the barest minimum: bread and jam and tea with some sort of sweetener and soup. Nor did they lay out energy and money on planning get-out plans. They knew they would not leave the ghetto alive and they planned no exit. Their aim was to avenge the helpless thousands who had gone undefended to their death; and to die with honour for the sake of human dignity and the good name of their people.

ŻOB prepared for partisan warfare. Events in January had shown that it was best to draw the Germans into dwelling houses where, in narrow corridors, on rooftops or stairways, the advantage belonged to the guerrilla force. They had also learnt that in the event of another surprise attack the fighters should not be separated from their main store of weapons. In summer 1942 the Germans had turned the ghetto into a huge workplace, organized into four main sections, and ŻOB now concentrated their fighting force in bases around these four areas. Mordecai Anielewicz commanded the central ghetto, Marek Edelman and the Bund were in charge of the brush-makers' area. He writes, 'The fighting groups live directly beside their points of operation. We are quartered like this so that we shall not be surprised by a German attack again and so that people get used to the spirit of being in the army, to army discipline and to being constantly in touch with our weapons.'[15]

People were building serious shelters now: a whole under-ground town existed beneath the ghetto, while routes were cleared across lofts and rooftops. Some shelters had sanitation and electricity. People were bedding in for a long siege. Encouraged by news of the German defeat at Stalingrad in winter 1942, they hoped that the tide of war would turn – and demoralized German soldiers were actually selling off their weapons. ŻOB too was stocking up, learning how to set mines and make Molotov cocktails. Cywia Lubetkin notes, 'During these intensive preparations for battle in Warsaw and other ghettos the Germans arrested and murdered dozens of our comrades who were . . . concerned with buying up weapons and transferring them from place to place, from ghetto to ghetto.'[16]

One of those arrested (on 6 March 1943) was a key figure in the Jewish underground, Arie (or Jurek) Wilner, ŻOB's representative on the Polish side of the wall who did major liaison work with the Polish underground.

A member of the Polish underground, Henryk Grabowski, wrote:

'All kinds of parcels and money for the ghetto began to pour into my place. I became a kind of "post box". In the meantime Jurek Wilner lived with me and kept in my room various explosives which, however, he didn't manage to smuggle into the ghetto. When it got "hot" at my place Jurek moved to another flat . . . That was where he was arrested. The flat had been under observation by the Gestapo . . . Jurek was caught entirely by chance instead of someone else. The situation was all the more serious because he had kept weapons, maps and various letters with surnames in the flat. The arrest took place – as Jurek told me himself – in the following way:

'When he came into the flat six Germans threw themselves on him, overpowered him and bound him. They then showed him everything that they had found during their inspection. On being questioned he confessed that they belonged to him. The Gestapo men beat him up and drove him by car to the HQ on Szucha Street. On the way one of them tried to question Jurek but he refused to give any evidence. So the German hit him in the face and said, "You'll sing out everything, we haven't had one of your kind before."

'Beaten to a pulp, Jurek lay on the concrete floor of a dungeon for three days . . . with swollen hands. Then the questioning started. They took him for an "Aryan". At the beginning they tried to persuade him that he's young, that he could save his life if he admitted the truth. Jurek however remained silent. The beating began. During the second time of questioning Jurek admitted that he was Jewish. Consternation ensued. They began detailed questioning: how had he got out of the ghetto and where had he got weapons from? Jurek continually replied, "I'm not connected with any organization . . . I want to avenge the death of my parents and that's why I've been keeping weapons." So then the torturers beat him up again and revived him every time he lost consciousness . . . In the end he totally passed out. When he came to he heard the words of one of his torturers: "Like talking to a brick wall . . ." They threw him back in the dungeon where he wanted to hang himself, afraid in case he might betray his comrades. But other Jews in his cell wouldn't let him do that, so he decided to starve himself to death and gave his food to his cellmates.

'Two and a half weeks later a selection was held . . . Wanting to hasten the end, Jurek attached himself to the group who had been sentenced. It turned out, however, that they had been led out not for execution but to forced labour.'[17]

Jurek Wilner was sent to a labour camp outside Warsaw. He got a message through to Henryk, who managed to rescue him from the camp. He took him to his flat and 'began to heal him with home cures'. His friends in the ghetto had given him up for dead. They were overjoyed to hear from contacts in the Polish underground that Jurek was still alive. They organized transport and Jurek, crippled by torture, went back to the ghetto to rejoin his friends in their impossible fight.

Great though the joy was at Jurek Wilner's return, his arrest had very serious consequences for ŻOB. All their good contacts on the Aryan side had collapsed. Precious time elapsed before the Polish underground became convinced that, even under extreme torture, Jurek had confessed to nothing. Many weeks passed before ŻOB received a cryptic phone call that a new courier should come. Cywia Lubetkin writes:

'It wasn't easy to find someone else to take Arie's place. Our people on the Aryan side risked their lives no less than in the ghetto, but they didn't want to be parted from their comrades, to cut themselves off from them completely, to live in a strange world which repudiated them all day, every day . . . After long and hard discussion two candidates were put forward, Mordecai Anielewicz and Yitzhak Zuckerman. The decision was made: Yitzhak Zuckerman would go to the Aryan side.'[18]

Six days later the last onslaught on the ghetto began.

Notes

1 *Memoirs.*
2 *Chronicle.*
3 *Extermination and Uprising.*
4 *Extermination.*
5 *Extermination.*
6 The description comes from Hanna Krall, *To Beat God to it!* (*Zdążyć przed Panem Bogiem*), Znak, Krakow, 1999.
7 *Chronicle.*
8 *Chronicle.*
9 *The Ghetto is Fighting.*
10 *Ghetto.*
11 *Extermination.*
12 *Extermination.*
13 *Extermination.*
14 *Extermination.*
15 *Ghetto.*
16 *Extermination.*
17 Henryk Grabowski, *My meeting with Jurek Wilner* in *Homeland.*
18 *Extermination.*

CHAPTER 8

The Uprising:
19 April–8 May 1943

On the night of 18 April 1943, the eve of Passover, the moon rose full and clear over Warsaw. The night was mild; the ghetto was vigilant. Cywia Lubetkin writes:

'At 2 a.m. . . . we were sitting down to our poor meal when . . . a comrade came in whose pale face showed us that something had happened. He came up to the table and said calmly that a moment ago news had come in from the Aryan side that the ghetto was going to be surrounded that night: the Germans would begin to attack at 6 a.m. . . . Our envoys ran quickly through the ghetto to warn people that dawn will be the beginning of our end. The elderly, women and children must hide. Young people – take up arms! . . . People crowd into bunkers . . . No one is visible now, it is as though everything which lived has been wiped from the face of the earth.'[1]

Marek Edelman, commander of the fighters at the brush-makers' factory compound reports:

'At 4 a.m. the Germans begin to make their appearance . . . arriving in small groups of three, four or five so as not to arouse the suspicions of ŻOB or the population . . . they form ranks, getting into regiments and companies. At 7 a.m. the motorized army appears in the ghetto – tanks and armoured cars. The Germans position their artillery outside. Now the SS are ready to attack . . . It appears as if their triumph is complete, as though the small handful of daredevil kids were afraid of this modern army, equipped and armed to perfection. As if these chits of boys had suddenly understood that there's no point in their wild goose chase . . .

'But no, we weren't frightened, nor were we surprised. We were simply waiting for the appropriate moment. It soon came. When the Germans had spread themselves out at the crossing of Miła and Zamenhof Streets, the groups of fighters barricaded at the four corners of the streets opened concentrated fire, as they say in military terminology. Fire exploded from unknown weapons (they were grenades we'd made ourselves), rounds of shots from automatic pistols tore the air (we had to save ammunition), rifles barked from somewhere further off. So it had begun.'[2]

There have been many unequal battles in history but few have been fought against such overwhelming odds. The young heroes in the ghetto held out to the end. There was no capitulation, no surrender, although the Nazis flung heavy weaponry, tanks, armoured cars and over 2,000 soldiers into the fight. The command of the German forces was transferred to General Stroop, who waged war as if he were fighting against a trained army. In addition, as Marek Edelman reports, as the fighting continued and German ambulances carried off their wounded, low-flying planes attacked the fighters from the air.

Shocked by Jewish armed resistance, the Germans split up into small groups and kept close to the walls. Several ghetto fighters record that the Germans did not dare venture into the street to collect their wounded.

Cywia Lubetkin writes:

'We had placed well-camouflaged mines on the main streets . . . We allowed the Germans to pass our positions, we let them through to the places which were mined. When they had gone, we switched on the current . . . Hardly had they marched through our position when a hail of bombs and grenades fell on their heads. They fell into a panic . . . We fought for many hours . . . Suddenly silence falls. The Germans are retreating . . . We are mad, drunk with victory. We cannot contain our joy. We hug and kiss one other . . . We hardly managed to snatch a rest when we heard our commander's whistle. The hum of motor engines had been heard from far off. The Germans were coming back. We took up our places at once. This time tanks appeared. We greeted them with grenades and Molotov cocktails. When the first tank burst into flames the Germans retreated. Another victory!'[3]

Marek Edelman writes:

'Hemmed in, the fighters defend themselves with tooth and nail, resisting the offensive with superhuman effort. They manage to get hold of two machine guns and many other weapons. A German tank is set on fire. That's the second one that day.

'By 2 o'clock in the afternoon there's not a single German anywhere in the ghetto. It's ŻOB's first complete victory over the Germans.'[4]

At nightfall the ghetto people left their hiding places. Everyone took stock of the day. After years of suffering victory was sweet.

Families gathered for the Seder (Passover) meal when the question is asked by the youngest member of the family: *Ma nishta-na ha-lajla ha-ze mi-kol ha-lejlot* – why is this night different from any other night? The young people knew and they had good cause to celebrate. Cywia Lubetkin writes how, reeling from weariness, she met up with her young comrades who filled a bath with hot water for her and insisted that she take a few moments to relax.

On the same evening soldiers from the Armia Krajowa (the

non-communist Home Army) attempted to make an opening in the ghetto wall. The attempt failed and two of the A.K. men were killed. The German command had feared the knock-on effect of the armed resistance in the ghetto might provoke a similar show of strength from the Poles, but the Polish underground was not yet ready to fight. The ghetto was left to fight alone.

The next day saw intense fighting in the workshops. Marek Edelman reports:

'. . . it was quiet until 2 p.m. It was only then that the Germans put in an appearance at the gateway into the brush-makers'. Once again they are closely grouped together. They don't know that at that very same moment our sentry put his hand on the electric switch . . . A mine which has been waiting for them for a long time explodes under the feet of the SS. Over 100 SS perish in the explosion, the rest retreat, seen off by shots from our fighters. The Germans wait another two hours before they try their luck again. Now they act differently, they go carefully, in single file in battle array and try to get into the brushmakers' compound . . . Out of 30 Germans who got into the compound, only a few get out again. The rest perish in the explosion of grenades and burning bottles. And again the Germans retreat from the ghetto. And the fighters celebrate their second complete victory.

'However the Germans don't give up and try to get into the compound from several sides. Everywhere they meet with decided resistance. The whole house is fighting. In one of the lofts we're suddenly surrounded. There are Germans close beside us in the same attic. There's no way we can get to the stairs. It's too dark in the recesses to see one another. We do not see that Sewek Dunski and Junghajzer have wormed their way down the steps from the loft and come up behind the Germans and are throwing grenades. We don't even notice how it happens that Michael Klepfisch has jumped straight on to the German automatic gun sticking out of the chimney. We only see that the way is clear. We find his body few hours later (when the Germans have been expelled). It is riddled like a sieve with two explosions from the automatic.'[5]

Thirty-year-old Michael Klepfisch was awarded the Cross of Military Virtue posthumously by the Polish government-in-exile. He is commemorated in Warsaw on the Path of Memory. His was an outstanding act; but the whole ghetto had become a theatre in which a drama of unprecedented courage was played out. Men, women and children in the hideouts and shelters resisted the Nazis to the death. The German command was forced to allude to 'the battle of the bunkers' in which starving civilians held off the soldiers of the Master Race.

On 21 April, the third day of the uprising, the Germans entered the ghetto in small groups. The fighters formed small mobile squads. Other groups and individuals fought alongside the Jewish Fighting Force. But the main fighting was still in the brushmakers' compound – and now the Germans resorted to a tactic which no one had expected: fire.

Marek Edelmann writes:

'Flames engulf the whole block instantly, black smoke chokes our throats, corrodes our eyes. The fighters have no intention of perishing alive in the flames. We stake everything on one hope and decide to get to the central ghetto whatever the cost. As we go the flames catch our clothes which begin to smoulder. Asphalt melts under our feet in a black sticky slime. Glass which has been scattered everywhere has turned into a stringy gooey mess which sticks to our feet as we walk. The heat of the burning pavement scorches the soles of our feet. We fight our way through the flames one after the other, from house to house, from yard to yard. We can't breathe. A hundred hammers pound inside our heads. Burning rafters fall around us. At last we get beyond the reach of the fire. We count it as happiness to stand on an inch of ground which isn't burning.

'Now the most difficult part remains. The only way into the central ghetto is through a small break in the wall which is guarded on three sides by military police, Ukrainians and Polish police. Twelve men guard the passage which is two metres wide – and five groups of fighters have to get through exactly at this point. One after the other, shoes bound with rags to muffle the sound of our footsteps . . . The Germans floodlight the spot . . . It looks as though no one else will get through. But with one shot Romanowicz extinguishes the spotlight. Before the Germans work out what's going on, we're all on the other side. There we join up with the groups of fighters over there – and continue the fight. It's almost as impossible to get about in this area too. Huge infernos often close entire streets. A sea of flames floods over the houses and yards. Wooden beams burn with a roar, walls crumble. There's no air. There is only black, caustic smoke and heavy, steaming heat. Heat beats from the flaming walls, from stairs which haven't caught light but are roasted to blackness.

'The all-powerful fire is now doing the thing the Germans couldn't do. Thousands of people are perishing in the flames . . . Hundreds of people end their lives by jumping from the third or fourth floor. Mothers save their children from being burnt alive by throwing them to the ground.'[6]

Yet still no one gave themselves up voluntarily to the enemy. People dug themselves deeper into their shelters – or took refuge in the sewers.

Seventeen-year-old Leon Najberg describes his basement hiding place:

'The young people grabbed a crowbar in order to try to force an opening in the chimney so that some air would get in. But after making this opening, fire swept in . . . The command was given to dampen our clothing and cover our face and hands with damp rags so that we could get through the fire . . . Around us we saw a sea of flames, thick clouds of smoke. I had the impression that I was in the middle of a burning oven in a bakery. The roar of burning houses mingled with the shouts of the wounded and women's laments.'[7]

A similar description comes from Cywia Lubetkin, who contrasts the hopeless scenes in the burning ghetto with the Polish side of the wall where people were celebrating the Easter holidays.

'The ghetto was burning. Flames surrounded it day and night. The fire consumed and destroyed every building. House after house, street after street turned into rubble. Pillars of fire rose into the air, shooting out sparks. A frightful red glow covered the sky.

'Nearby, on the other side of the wall, life flowed on as usual, as yesterday, as always. People, citizens of the capital, enjoyed themselves. They saw the smoke from the fires by day and the flames by night. A carousel went round and round beside the ghetto, children danced in a circle. It was charming. They were happy. Country girls visiting the capital rode on the roundabout, looking over at the flames of the ghetto . . . The wind blew soot from smoking houses into their nostrils. Shooting sparks sometimes got across the wall and set fire to houses, but there the fire was put out at once while no one hurried to bring help to the ghetto. Everything was ablaze and there was no one to put it out.'[8]

Jews in hiding on the other side of the wall watched the ghetto burn; they were trying to stay incognito, they had to conceal their sorrow – and often had to listen to wounding remarks. The following memoir comes from an album of pre-war photographs published recently in Warsaw. The author of this extract, Eugenia, or Gina, Gnoińska incurred her grand-mother's disfavour when she married a Catholic Pole. For a long time she had no word of her family. Eventually her brother-in-law, after great effort, managed to find their whereabouts in the ghetto. Gina sent them money and received a letter back:

'"Dear, darling Gina! The Lord God must have inspired you to send those 300 zloties. The gentleman who brought the money found us in our beds in the doorway – although our landlord was Jewish he had thrown us out of the flat because we're owing three months' rent. There's even some left over to buy half a loaf of bread. May the Lord God grant you life!

'"Granny is dying and asks us to tell you that you're not under a curse any more. She blesses you and your little son and prays you will both live to see better days. Dad is at the wash-tub, washing our linen in cold water without soap. He's doing it because none of us is able to any more. Little Dawidek starved to death. I hope you live to see better times but you can imagine what will become of us. Don't give us your address."

'I read and wept, read and learnt it all off by heart because I knew the time would come when I would have to destroy that letter. And one day our neighbours knocked at our door. "Please ma'am, may we have a look through your window at the way the Jews are burning in the ghetto?" I was really shaken because, after all, their windows looked out the same side as ours. I threw that letter from Franka on the fire at once, and my mum's gold locket as well, with her photograph taken in the garden in 1907. I regret that to this day . . . but I'd lost my head. I went back into the room and there was a lively conversation going on. "O, how they're burning! Their side-locks are sizzling! And what do you think about it, Mrs Gnoińska? Don't you think it's good that Hitler's getting rid of the Jews?" I wanted to laugh with them but before my eyes came my father doing the washing and I heard him say, "You won't tell them, my daughter." So I replied, "No, Mr Budrewicz, I'm not going to laugh because there's nothing to laugh at. They'll do the same to us Poles as soon as they've finished with them."[9]

As the ghetto was engulfed in flames carefully made hideouts became death-traps; carefully hoarded provisions perished. The Nazis used specially trained dogs to sniff out signs of human life, listening devices to catch the murmur of conversation, a child's cry – and also had informers who indicated where the hideouts were. Some did this after torture; others believed Nazi promises that if they informed they would be safe. Broken physically though people were, living in indescribable condi-tions, very few answered these appeals. They had to be dragged out to look their last on the pale, drawn faces of their children, their parents, husbands, wives, sweethearts, friends – and the mocking gaze of their executioners who shot defenceless people in the bright spring sunlight.

Late April and early May 1943 were bright and sunny – but the people in the burning ghetto hid underground only ever saw darkness. A few ŻOB fighters, risking their lives, stayed above ground, keeping watch, ready to attack. Everyone else was squashed into underground bunkers, cramped so closely together that if one person wanted to turn over, everyone else had to turn over too. There was no way anyone could cook. No one had tasted bread for days. At night, under cover of darkness, people crept out of their underground lairs, stretched

Don't go to Uncle's Wedding

their limbs, heated soup – no need to worry about cooking fires being seen when the whole air was full of smoke. They met up with families and friends and shared news. Another day of life had been granted to them and they could relax, for the Germans did not dare comb the ghetto by night. At daybreak the long silent vigil in the dark began all over again. The longing for sunlight and the real world produced a strange melancholia in the ghetto.

The ŻOB command were offered refuge in a bunker below 18 Miła Street. This extensive hideout had been skilfully constructed by leading lights in the ghetto's criminal under-world. The bunker had water and electricity, a kitchen, a toilet and even a meeting room. The 'king' of this underworld, Shmul Asher, warmly welcomed Mordecai Anielewicz and the Fighting Force. 'We are entirely at your disposal,' he assured them. And indeed the young fighters with their high principles found that the shady characters from the world of crime were expert guides, climbing over rooftops and crawling with ease through cellars. At night the 'king' pulled on boots which had been shone to perfection by one of his minions and left his hiding place through an exit which had been built wide enough to accommodate his immense frame. 'He slimmed down as time went on,' Cywia Lubetkin remarks, 'and the exit became too wide for him.'[10]

In this bunker were 120 fighters, including Mordecai Anielewicz, his girlfriend Mira, Arie (Jurek) Wilner and others as well as the 'king', his minions and other civilians.

The ghetto was in its death throes and the Fighting Force leadership debated what to do. Someone mentioned that a person in the hideout on Franciszańska Street where the remnants of Marek Edelman's brushmakers' fighting squad was based might act as a guide through the sewers. It was decided that

Cywia Lubetkin and a few others should find out more details.

It took a long time to cross the ruins in the dark and then wait for the outcome of a reconnoitre through the sewers. By now it was almost daybreak, the morning of 8 May. Cywia and her party wanted to make their way back to 18 Miła Street and debrief. But it was impossible to cross the ghetto by day. They had to wait until nightfall before they began the hazardous route back to 18 Miła Street. But once there, their hearts sank. There were six concealed entrances into the bunker – and they seemed to have disappeared. No one answered the password. They searched around in the ruins, becoming more and more certain that a terrible tragedy had taken place. Then they spotted 'misty silhouettes' and saw their comrades. 'Completely covered in mud and blood, weakened and shaking, they looked like phantoms, not people . . . Some were unconscious, others hardly breathed. Jehuda Węgrower from Ha-Shomer ha-Za'ir was coughing up blood. Tosia Altman was lying with wounds in her head and legs.'[11]

And now, from the few survivors they heard what had happened. The ŻOB Command was dead. Marek Edelman reports:

'On 8 May ŻOB's main Command is surrounded by divisions of Germans and Ukrainians. There follow two hours' heavy fighting. When the Germans see that they're not going to conquer the bunker in fair fight they throw gas bombs inside. Those who are not killed by German bullets, those who are not poisoned by gas, take their own lives. It's clear that there's no way out but it doesn't cross anyone's mind to give themselves up alive into German hands. Jurek Wilner calls the fighters to collective suicide . . . In this way 80 per cent of the surviving fighters perish, the ŻOB Commander Mordecai Anielewicz among them.'[12]

Cywia Lubetkin describes the end more fully. The attack had come in the afternoon when everyone was lying half naked on the floor or on benches. Suddenly the sentry gave word that Germans were approaching. The usual German tactic was to appeal to people to come out, persuading them that they would be unharmed. About 60 civilians answered this appeal. The ŻOB fighters responded with fire. And, as Marek Edelman reports, the Germans responded with gas. Cywia says that at first they let in just a small amount of gas, enough to weaken the fighters. Death was inescapable and Arie Wilner had cried out, 'Don't give yourselves into their hands.' He had shot himself and then a series of shots had rung out throughout the bunker. Some who had been wounded and could no longer hold weapons, or whose weapons failed, begged their comrades to shoot them. Suddenly someone found an exit which the Germans had missed. The few survivors who now told the story had got out that way, some wounded after their suicide attempts, all poisoned by gas. It is not clear exactly how Mordecai Anielewicz had met his end. Cywia writes that he was, 'loved by everyone, a valiant leader, a charming, beautiful young boy who had a smile on his lips even in moments of danger'.[13]

Shocked, grief-stricken, the small group of fighters tried to gain entrance to the bunker, but there was no way in. So now they had to find a place of safety for their wounded comrades. Full of sorrow, they left 18 Miła Street. 'Our lips whispered words of farewell. We were leaving our fallen, heroic comrades and burying our last hopes and dreams . . . They were all left here, under the ruins. We walked like a row of living corpses, moving, lifeless shadows,' wrote Cywia Lubetkin.[14]

They took the only route left: through the sewers. Marek Edelman describes the scene:

'The way through the sewers lasts the whole night. We keep stumbling upon barricades of barbed wire in the sewers – German sappers have probably done this in anticipation. The manholes are covered over with rubble. Grenades hang in the passages and will explode at once as soon as they're touched. Every so often the Germans let in poison gas. In these conditions, in sewers 70 cm high, where it's not possible to stand at full height and the water reaches to our mouths, we wait 48 hours at the exit. Every moment someone faints. Most of all we're tormented by thirst. Some people drink the thick, sludgy sewer water. Seconds last for hours.

'On 10 May at 10 a.m. two lorries drive up to the manhole cover . . . In broad daylight, without any armed guards (the promised cover from A.K. has let us down) . . . the manhole cover is opened and Jews with weapons in their hands come out of the black hole one after the other in front of an astonished crowd (at that time the mere sight of a Jew is a sensation). The people haven't all managed to get out. Powerfully, heavily the manhole cover crashed shut and the lorries take off at full speed.'[15]

It was the end. 'There is no longer a Jewish residential area in Warsaw,' wrote General Stroop to his superiors – and blew up the main synagogue in Tlomackie Street to emphasize his victory. The Nazi general was caught in a dilemma. He had to explain why he had taken so long and used so much armed power to overcome the ghetto – but he had to minimize Jewish resistance: the 'subhuman underclass' was not supposed to have qualities of courage, leadership, humanity.

The entire ghetto was reduced to a pile of rubble. Not one building stood higher than the second floor. However, incredibly, right until September people still hid in underground cavities – and the Germans still hunted them out.

Slave labourers were sent from concentration camps to gather bricks from the ruins. The blasted ghetto also became a place of execution for Jews caught in hiding. The Nazis boasted of it as a symbol of a great victory, but for one German soldier at least it was a matter of shame. Captain Wilm Hosenfeld's wartime diary has survived. He wrote:

'The entire ghetto has been razed by fire. These brutes think we shall win the war that way. But we have lost the war with this appalling mass murder of the Jews. We have brought shame upon ourselves that cannot be wiped out; it's a curse that can't be lifted. We deserve no mercy; we are all guilty.'[16]

The end of the war was still two years away but Jewish life had been already virtually exterminated. The few who survived did so in hiding; the next chapter recounts their experiences.

Notes

1 *Extermination and Uprising.*
2 *The Ghetto is Fighting.*
3 *Extermination.*
4 *Ghetto.*
5 *Ghetto.*
6 *Ghetto.*
7 *Memoirs.*
8 *Extermination.*
9 Golda Tencer, *And Still I See Their Faces: Images of Polish Jews*, Shalom Foundation, Warsaw, 1998.
10 *Extermination.*
11 *Extermination.*
12 *Ghetto.*
13 *Extermination.*
14 *Extermination.*
15 *Ghetto.*
16 W. Szpilman, *The Pianist*, Gollancz, London, 1999.

CHAPTER 9

In hiding

In the barbarous chessboard of war ordinary people, including children, are caught in dilemmas which continue long after the signing of peace. Maria Kamińska was born Jewish with a different name. It was changed when she was five when, in order to save her life, her parents gave her away. 'I'm an old woman now,' she wrote, 'but still I feel increasingly that someone stole my name and with it my whole life.'[1]

Although giving help to Jews was punishable by death, many Polish people hid Jews. Hiding people long term was not only dangerous, it was costly, it involved ingenuity: the person who went shopping for food mustn't be seen to buy more than usual; neighbours mustn't have cause to guess that there was someone hiding in the cellar, in the attic, behind the cupboard. And if it was hard for adults to lie in the dark with nothing to do for days, weeks, months on end – how much more for children!

Krystyna, who was eight when war broke out, lived in an underground hideout:

'We had three openings in the bunker and on sunny days it was a bit brighter, but when it was cloudy it was completely dark. We lay like that for days and nights. In spring when the snow melted water poured in on us and soaked everything, and in the winter we froze . . . We were so hungry that none of us could walk any more. In the end the peasant woman refused even to give us water. Then my brother went out one night and drank water from a puddle and died. We buried him in the forest at night. My uncle left the bunker once and was never seen again. We sat hidden like that for 18 months until the Russians came. I couldn't walk at all and I still have very weak legs, while Roza is always sad, she often cries and doesn't want to play with other children.'[2]

Another child, aged five at the beginning of the war, recalls:

'I didn't see the light of day for six months. That's why I wear glasses now. I wasn't allowed to walk about in case people heard me . . . The lady of the house came three times a day with food and spoke to me really quietly but she couldn't stay long because her mother-in-law was such a bad woman she would have gone to the Gestapo at once . . .'[3]

Fryda Koch sums up the thoughts of many children when she says, 'I can tell you now what we went through, but I don't know how to describe the things we felt.'[4]

The risks were enormous and most people had to change hiding places over and over again: a neighbour might have become suspicious, a member of the household might break down, terrified of Nazi reprisals; and many children and adults express the overwhelming sense of loneliness they experienced as they were in hiding. Normal life flowed by but they could only observe it through chinks in the curtains, cracks in the walls. 'There was a crack between the curtain and the wall and I remember how I peeked through and how miserable I was as I watched children playing outside,' wrote Alexandria Berłowicz.[5]

Adam Pruszkowski from Warsaw was hidden in an orphanage which consisted of a hundred boys, divided into three groups, each looked after by a nun. He writes:

'I was an only child and until the moment I had left the

ghetto I had never been parted from my parents . . . I was afraid of everybody and of everything. I wasn't afraid of the nuns, I knew that they would save me and I didn't experience anything bad from them. I was really afraid of the other boys, thinking they might betray me. They knew that I was some-one different, a Jew, and therefore someone condemned to death. I learnt that very quickly. I knew that I wasn't allowed to say anything about myself just as I knew I mustn't get undressed in front of anyone . . . Paralysed with fear and timidity I didn't make friends with anyone . . .'[6]

Many children had witnessed the deaths of their close family. Rena Kant was ten when she was awakened by a Jewish police-man and told to go to the market square.

'Mummy wasn't there, only my nine-year-old sister and my four-year-old brother . . . I took my brother and told my sister to come with me and we would hide. I knew that they were going to deport us and murder us and I didn't want to go to the market. But my sister was afraid to move anywhere and she didn't go with me. My little brother and I went through the garden . . . I was quite calm and I carried my brother in my arms because he had had rickets and couldn't walk or talk . . . I wandered around the fields and villages all day. Peasants gave us some food. I thought I'd meet up with Mummy because she often went out to the village but Mummy didn't appear and I have never seen her since . . . I asked some peasants to help us and they let us come in, gave us food and put us up for the night even though they knew that we were Jewish. I searched for my auntie and found her (and Granny) at a forester's. Auntie couldn't lead Granny about any more. Granny gave herself up to the police. I was told to go on with Auntie. Auntie said I couldn't keep on carrying my brother. I was really very tired. I had been carrying him all day. My brother was heavy and I wasn't strong enough. Now (I'm older) I would be able to carry him longer. I left him outside a house in the village. He cried when I went away. I thought that someone might take him in. Fries told me that a child had been shot in Krosno. An SS man called Becker had shot him. My conscience pricks me sometimes because I'd left him behind, but I really couldn't carry him any more.'[7]

Krystyna Budnicka was the sole survivor of eight children. Her story is as follows:

'Our family was patriarchal, religious, we kept all the requirements of the Law of Moses. I still remember festive Sabbath evenings around our big table, with my father with his beautiful long silver beard "reigning" at the head . . . My happy childhood ended with the outbreak of war in 1939. I was seven . . .

'I can remember the events of those years quite clearly but most of all I remember the fear which totally overcame me, the beating of my heart, clenching my fists on Mum's dress until they were sore as I clung despairingly to her . . . Two of my brothers were taken to Treblinka with their wives and children . . . After July 1942 my brothers . . . began to build a bunker . . . connected to a sewer by means of a tunnel several metres deep. It took several months to build . . . We moved in a few months before the Uprising. In the bunker there were about 20 people over and above our family, and as far as children were concerned, there were two of us, my 13-year-old brother and I (11 years old). Three of my brothers were members of the Jewish Fighting Force and took an active part in the Uprising. We survived in the bunker during the whole Uprising and when it was over my brothers returned to the bunker. Everything was burning round about – the temperature in the bunker was very high and to cool off we went into the sewer, but the Germans let in gas and corpses floated along the canals.

In hiding

The first days and weeks were dreadful . . . We had to escape to the canal over and over again, squeezing through the narrow tunnel. (I still relive these flights in nightmares all these years after the war.) There was no light or water in the bunker at that time. Many people in our bunker didn't last out and went out of the sewer straight into the bullets of Germans who were waiting by the manhole . . . Thus we lived for many months until even our hunger rations finished and we had to make contact with the outside world . . . I don't know which organization helped us but it was organized help.

'The first, unfortunately, to leave the bunker was my brother Raphael – he had a serious illness (typhus or dysentery). We were left without his leadership and a disaster occurred – the bunker was discovered . . . Two of my brothers, Isaak and Chaim, died then but the rest of us, hastily and in a panic, managed to hide in the sewer. There were my parents who were very weak and ill, my sister, sister-in-law, youngest brother and me . . . We sat on boards in the sewer for 48 hours before we contacted the world above and informed them of our situation. People came for us by night but it turned out that 'our' manhole had been soldered up. We had to go through to another exit – through a sewer where the water flowed in a fast current. The current tore at us – it was difficult to stand on such very weak legs . . . My parents weren't strong enough. They stayed beside the soldered up exit and my 23-year-old sister Pola stayed with them – she didn't want to leave them alone. Mum said "You must go! Raphael is there, he will have organized help for sure." But no help was organized and they stayed in the sewer for ever.

'But I got out after nine months living in the bunker. There were still four of us . . . and our whole foursome were living corpses. They carried us out, none of us could stand up by ourselves. Packed into sacks we were carried like luggage to our hiding place. We lived in the cellar of a burnt-out building. They began to feed us but unfortunately my little brother died . . . We three were left. Raphael got involved in work with the underground. Having had experience, he began to build a tunnel to the sewer to be ready for the next Uprising . . . My brother was betrayed to the Germans by a person whom he'd trusted . . . Raphael died in January 1944 in the torture chamber on Szucha Avenue – without betraying the place where my sister-in-law and I were living. So we were left alone now – my sister-in-law and I . . . Many different people looked after us. I don't know their names or which organization they represented. We received money every month for our food. I don't know where it had come from. The last time it was brought by a courier named Zosia in the early hours of the morning on 1 September 1944. That afternoon the (Warsaw) Uprising broke out . . . and we were evacuated with everyone else . . . My sister-in-law decided that it would be safer for me to be in a group of other children. Our helper asked some nuns to take me. They did so, although there wasn't a shadow of doubt as to my origins, especially as I had no documents to show. My sister-in-law . . . was transported to Germany for forced labour. She survived the war.

'And I, in an orphanage among other children (several were Jewish), awaited the end of the Occupation, thanks to the care of the nuns who protected me. I was a very grown-up 13-year-old person.'[8]

People in hiding depended on a whole chain of people and events for their safety – but it took only a single voice to give everyone away; close neighbours were often the people least to be trusted. The ingenuity and endurance necessary to survive were often almost superhuman. Dr Emanuel Ringelblum sums up the tensions and problems of Polish 'guardian angels' who hid Jews. Typically, he sets the problem in a wider social context, but the story he tells is his own, and the people in the hiding place included himself, his wife, Judyta and their 14-year-old son, Uri:

'The life of a Pole who hides a Jew is not the easiest. The whole country is gripped by mad terror . . . The best part of society, the most noble and self-sacrificial elements have been deported *en masse* to concentration camps and prisons. Spying and denunciation are rife . . . There are arrests and round-ups at every turn. The masses are poisoned with anti-Semitism which pours from the press and radio every day. In this kind of atmosphere of unrest and terror, of passivity and indifference, hiding Jews . . . is a very difficult thing. A Jew in anyone's flat . . . is dynamite which can explode at any moment and blow up the whole flat.'[9]

At the end of February 1943 Dr Ringelblum had escaped from the Warsaw ghetto with his family but he returned to the ghetto on the eve of the Uprising. He was then captured and deported to an SS camp. For several months there was no news of him, but in July 1943 word came of his whereabouts through a member of Żegota, the Council for the Aid of Jews. Theodore Pajewski, an underground officer in the Armia Krajowa, was employed as a railway worker and used this position to rescue people and pass on information. With the help of a Jewish girl, Roza Kossower, he rescued the ghetto historian and smuggled him back to Warsaw. Theodore Pajewski himself perished in a prison camp in Germany in 1944.

Dr Ringelblum then went into hiding with his family. He nicknames his hideout 'Miss Chrissie', from the Polish word for a hiding place. He pays generous tribute to the Marczak family who hid him and 33 others:

'The helm of the hideout is held in the hands of the chief, Władysław M, aged 37, a gardener. He decided to save dozens of Jews despite the sentence of death the Occupier had passed on them. Władysław is committed body and soul to his dearest "love", Miss Chrissie. He thinks about her by day and dreams about her by night . . . Władysław is exceptionally brave. When he had to save Chrissie's present tenants from the ghetto he personally drove his cart to his goal, loaded cases and packages on to the cart, sat the people on top and drove off home . . . Mrs M is a true mother to Chrissie. She can't sleep at night because of her. She goes to see her early in the morning to make sure everything is all right. She watches over Chrissie and shares her joys and sorrows . . . Mrs M is Chrissie's heart, Władysław is the brain and Mrs M's grandson Mariusz is Chrissie's eyes, her guardian angel and inseparable comrade. His function is very simple but 34 people depend for their lives on it. Mariusz brings Chrissie food, carries out slop-buckets and, most important, he watches over her all the hours God sends to make sure nobody gets too close.'[10]

Dr Ringelblum carried on his academic work in his hiding place. A coded report of this work was carried by courier to London on 1 March 1944 and sent out to the Jewish Academic Institute in New York. Six days later Chrissie was betrayed. Emanuel and Judyta Ringelblum, their son Uri and all the other people caught in hiding were taken to the ruins of the ghetto and shot. Władysław Marczak and Mariusz were executed with them, along with another friend, Mieczyslaw Wolski. Indeed, as Ringelblum had put it, 'The life of a Pole who hides a Jew is not the easiest' – and nor was the death.[11]

So why did some Polish people help their Jewish neighbours even to the point of laying down their lives while others watched mistreatment and murder in silence – or even aided

In hiding

and abetted the Nazis? The whole discussion lies outside the
scope of this book but when Pope John Paul paid the first
Papal visit to the Eastern bloc in 1979 he said, 'I ask you to
accept . . . the whole of the spiritual legacy which goes with the
name "Poland".' That legacy includes the Jews of Poland, their
history – and their relationships with their Polish neighbours.

The first Jews came to Poland in the aftermath of persecution in medieval Europe. As merchants and traders they were
readily granted asylum by the Polish king. Jewish rights were
uniquely protected by the Statute of Kalisz (1264). An old
legend says that Jews found an immediate affinity to Poland:
the name sounded like the Hebrew imperative *po lin* – 'rest
here'.

Unfortunately, despite some enlightened monarchs, Jewish
safety always depended on economic and political pressures.
None the less, Jewish social, cultural and religious life flourished in three languages, Hebrew, Yiddish and Polish. Polish
Jewry, rich in spiritual learning, was the birthplace of Hasidism.
The Baal Shem Tov, the great Hasidic master, inspired a movement which brought the Shekinah – the glory of the Most
High – into the small towns of Poland and infused the hard-
ships of every day life with festive joy.

In 1795 Poland was partitioned between Russia, Austria and
Prussia and only re-emerged as a nation in 1918 under Marshal
Piłsudski, who was broadly socialist and tried to float the idea
of a pluralist Poland. Economic recession, however, began to
put great pressure on Jewish life. After Piłsudksi's death in 1935
the National Democratic Party was blatantly anti-Semitic,
excluding Jews from most branches of higher education and
carrying out acts of violence on Jewish property.

In pre-war Poland 75 per cent of what we might nowadays
call 'ethnic' Poles lived in the country while 75 per cent of all

Jews lived in cities and small towns. They tended to run shops – often employing only one person – and small workshops. Fifty-three per cent of all tailors were Jewish and 40 per cent of all shoemakers. So the typical points of contact between Poles and Jews were commercial: Jews made – and Poles paid. Often there was complete satisfaction and harmony on both sides – and it was frequently this sort of good relationship which led to Poles giving what aid and assistance they could to their afflicted Jewish acquaintances; but the reverse was also true: the very visible Jewish presence in trade, however small, could become a source of tension. Moreover, traditionally in Poland, Jews had been employed by the landowning nobility to collect the rents from peasant farmers. Toll booths into the city were also manned by Jews. A peasant who had had a bad day at the market easily projected his resentment on to the bearded man in a black gaberdine who had taken his few *grosze* as he had entered the city that morning – and later, tragically, allow those bad feelings to override any sense of neighbourly help.

But there were cases when the plight of Jews under the Nazis caused previously avowedly anti-Semitic people to take positive and heroic action in defence of Jewish life. The writer Zofia Kossak has already been mentioned, and in *Memoirs of the Warsaw Ghetto*, Dr Grynberg includes a little piece called *Rebirth* by Henryk Ryszewski who, with the help of his wife and son, hid Jewish families in his Warsaw flat:

'Bearing someone else's collective torment and living under the weight of it I had to be reborn. A calf once sought refuge with Rabbi Yehudah Hamnassi but he handed it over to the butcher's knife, saying, "Go to the slaughter – you were created for this." The Rabbi suffered for many years because of this and when a servant girl wanted to drown kittens he called out with

sorrow, "Leave them, since the Lord is merciful to all his crea-
tures." And from that day his sufferings ceased. My sickness,
which was called anti-Semitism, was long and drawn-out, but
I was cured suddenly when I showed mercy to others in the
Name of Our Lord and took them under my roof."[12]

Some people survived like castaways, scavenging food, living
on their wits. Władysław Szpilman had been snatched from
his family as they were about to board the death wagons – his
escape is told in Chapter 6. Thereafter he survived thanks to
amazing inner resourcefulness, physical endurance – and a
series of miracles. The last person to help him was, incredibly,
a German officer. Władysław Szpilman's story of his encounter
with Captain Wilm Hosenfeld makes *The Pianist* one of the
most remarkable books to have come out of the Warsaw ghetto.
As the officer guided the starving outcast to safety Szpilman
ventured to ask, 'Are you German?' 'Yes, I am!' Hosenfeld
admitted. 'And ashamed of it, after everything that's been
happening.' Władysław Szpilman's account continues:

'On 12 December the officer came for the last time. He
brought me a larger supply of bread than before and a warm
eiderdown. He told me he was leaving Warsaw with his
detachment, and I must on no account lose heart, since the
Soviet offensive was expected any day now. "In Warsaw?"
"Yes." "But how will I survive the street fighting?" I asked
anxiously. "If you and I have survived this inferno for over five
years," he replied, "it's obviously God's will for us to live. Well,
we have to believe that, anyway."'[13]

A deeply believing Christian, Hosenfeld had used his position in charge of a sports stadium to save endangered people.
Arrested in 1945, he was transported to a prison camp in the
Soviet Union where he died in 1952, his body and mind broken
from harsh treatment and beatings. His life of personal faith,

unselfishness and courage received no reward, but in the Avenue of the Just in Jerusalem a tree will honour his memory.

In the ghetto, in the death trains, in the face of death itself, people lost – or found – faith in life, in humanity, in God. This will be the subject of the next chapter.

Notes

1 *Children*.
2 Krystyna Gold in *Accuse*.
3 Regina Ruck in *Accuse*.
4 *Accuse*.
5 *Children*.
6 *Children*.
7 Rena Kant in *Accuse*.
8 *Children*.
9 *Homeland*.
10 *Homeland*.
11 *Homeland*.
12 *Memoirs*.
13 W. Szpilman, *The Pianist*, Gollancz, London 1999.

CHAPTER 10

The hard silence of God

It is said that before a scribe started to copy the Law he had to cleanse himself with a ritual bath. Then, as he bent over the page, his pen poised, he had to steady the trembling of his hand and heart: the slightest mistake would mean the destruction of the entire work.

Emanuel Ringelblum, the chronicler of the Warsaw ghetto, noted the death of a friend and wrote:

'When he visited me he looked at the list of those who had been killed and added a few names. Now the name of Yitzhak Giterman figures in the same list . . . My hand trembles as I write these words because who knows if some future historian, looking at the record, will not write my name too, "E. Ringelblum".'[1]

Hands tremble and words fail. Yet in the extreme circumstances of the ghetto, of *Umschlagplatz*, the death trains, there was unbelief and there was also the deepest trust. Beyond – and even within – the evil the Nazi regime unleashed, people showed self-sacrificing love, immeasurable courage, humanity stretched to its ultimate limits. An eyewitness describes prayer during air raids over the ghetto:

'Darkness, rain, white figures, choral prayers, singing to the accompaniment of gunfire. O, Jehovah, look on your people, we cry to You. Do you see our torments, O, great and powerful God? You led us out of the land of the pharaohs on whom you

113

put your curse, you avenged us with ten plagues, you fed us with manna. You who are almighty, perform a miracle now, set us free and punish our tyrants.'[2]

Hearing a mass execution, Leon Najberg records the response of those with whom he was in hiding:

'Their pure, unspotted souls had flown away and were circling above us, living Jews, with a silent accusation on their lips which had stiffened from blood . . . We didn't heed the danger we were in, we all wept together, and . . . said 'Kaddish' for the souls of those who had been so tragically murdered, lamenting as we did so and weeping.'[3]

Many people died with the Holy Name on their lips. Calel Perechodnik, a member of the Jewish Police, describes how three colleagues were led away to be executed. One was severely beaten: 'In the end, he was thrown, half unconscious into the ditch. Before his death the unfortunate man managed to shout out in Hebrew, "Hear, O Israel, the Lord our God, the Lord is One".'[4]

Twenty-six-year-old Calel Perechodnik was a victim of the Holocaust – and a participant in its crimes. His memoir shows what it is like to live with loss: the loss of dear ones, the loss of faith, the loss of self-respect.

'I don't believe in any democratic slogans. Man has a sleeping devil within himself – and he will have him in heaven too. I lived among Poles for 26 years and the devil slept, but when circumstances were favourable he awoke and showed his hellish countenance.'[5]

Perechodnik pours out a personal confession, but expects no pardon:

'I do not ask for absolution; if I believed in God, Paradise, Hell, in a reward or a punishment after death – I wouldn't have written (this memoir) . . . I saw with my own eyes the decline of Polish Jewry against the background of the burning Warsaw ghetto . . . I understood the hopelessness of the battle, I grasped the fact that sooner or later I too will have to share the fate of the Jews . . . It was then, on 7 May 1943, that I decided to write my memoirs.'[6]

With harrowing precision he describes the terrible day in which he conducted his wife and child to the town square of Otwock, near Warsaw, to await the death train. It was his daughter's second birthday. Eight thousand unarmed people sat in the square surrounded by 200 men with guns – and no one tried to resist:

'The wagons are approaching. O, God, perform a miracle! We (the Police) turn to the Germans, almost on our knees we beg for mercy for our wives. The Germanic Devil continues to mock us, "Okay, they'll be set free," they assure us. I fly to my wife on wings of joy. "Anka, Anka," I cry, "you're saved!" . . . The group of (police) wives is moved to one side at last. They order us to load the remaining people into the wagons . . . We work briskly, there's no demon of protest mastering us now, nor even pity for the remaining Jews . . . The police lead their own fathers and mothers to the trucks, they themselves bolt the doors as if with their own hands they were hammering nails into their coffins for all eternity . . . The tempo of work is wild. There's pressure above our eyes, and unbearable pain in our hearts and one thought in our heads, namely, that in a moment we'll collect our wives and children and flee from this accursed square. It's already twilight, already everyone has been loaded. The Germans come across to the police wives and begin to segregate them. The children are not to be set free . . . Almost out of my mind I grab little Aluska, bone of my bone, blood of my blood and put her on one side. She stands alone, hungry, sleepy, surprised. Perhaps she doesn't

115

understand why Father, who is always so good to her, is leaving her in the darkness. She stands and doesn't cry, only her eyes shine, those eyes, those big eyes. Suddenly we see that the Germans are turning their guns on us. The order is given: "All policemen to the other end of the square, quick march! Group in two rows!" We think we're standing stock still, but no, against our will our legs carry us to the other side of the square . . . From afar I see only a cloud of dust and silhouettes which I cannot differentiate. Everything is lost. Hurry, now, policemen – executioners of your own wives and children – offer them a last service, give them bread through the little windows of the wagons. No one can say that the Germans stint the Jews on bread. A long whistle – O, Anka, you have set out on your last journey. O, God, be merciful to me!'[7]

Perechodnik questions: 'Does God exist, is there some form of higher righteousness who governs this world. If so, then why is he silent? Why do thunderbolts not fall from the sky, why does the earth not open and swallow up the executioners of women and children?' And, aware of his own guilt, he adds, 'What are we to do, poor victims of our own vileness?'[8]

Many people asked, 'Where is God?' Some envied those who still believed:

'Those who believe are lucky. They can bow their head humbly or lift their eyes to heaven and beg, "Through all our sufferings, our torments of hopeless longing and pain without solace, through countless humiliations . . . we ask You, Lord, to remove the burden from our shoulders and make us become people once more" . . . It is hard for us who do not believe. We cannot soothe our heavy hearts by prayer, nor entrust our worries to someone who will save us from them.'[9]

Yitzhak Katzenelson, the poet mentioned by Cywia Lubetkin, laments a massacre on Miła Street.

'There is this street in Warsaw, Miła Street . . . Who is weeping? Not I. Weeping has fallen silent within me. Miła Street surpasses any tears . . . There is this street in Warsaw. There is this street, you know, but there is no God, that's fine . . . Although it's bad without him . . . how bad it is we already know today.

'But if he existed – that's frightful! God – and Miła Street . . . What a pair, the two of them! O, get your children out of your cases and batter them against the wall! Throw yourselves into the fire and tear your hair! And wring your hands impotently: There is a God! O, what an injustice! O, what unearthly shame! Indescribable mockery!'[10]

Another poem by an unknown author, entitled, *Where is God?* was found in the Ringelblum archives.

'There, where heaven used to be, the Jews are walking to death in obedient order. The Tablets are broken – the Law is trodden underfoot. All around are darkness and greyness. The people are perishing – the executioners' commands are unnecessary. Where is God?'[11]

Some people met sufferings with simple faith. A mother tried to defend her daughter who was being raped by a guard. Now she is dying, her head beaten in by the guard's rifle butt, and a memoir writer reproduces her last words:

'My child, the end has come . . . You will be an orphan, but you must know that God is in heaven. It is not we who order our own lives, God rules over us. Such is his will. He is the best Father, the most trustworthy guardian. He will never let you down. You can always trust him wherever you go. When everyone else abandons you, he is the only one who will not leave you . . . Live in God, have him always in your heart . . . Remember, love the world and love people because God has created them. He knows what he is doing.'[12]

In his book *Text in the Face of Extermination*, Dr Jan Leociak discusses these texts and highlights a diary by a dental technician, Karol Rotgeber, who escaped from the ghetto on 15 February 1943. From his hiding place Rotgeber watched the burning ghetto and, like Calel Perechodnik, decided to write his memoirs. Like Perechodnik, Rotgeber cries to the silent heavens – but, unlike Perechodnik, he does not blaspheme nor deny God – although he challenges his absence. Dr Leociak writes that he 'tunes his voice to the melody of Jeremiah's Lamentations'. Rotgeber's diaries, which are in the Ringelblum archives, consist of 15 handwritten exercise books. Each text is dedicated to his son, 13-year-old Paweł, who had been deported on 18 August 1942, and begins with an appeal to God to restore righteousness to the earth. 'Why, O God, do you give the blood of the most innocent to Moloch?' he asks. 'Where is the conscience of the world? The only sound to be heard is the tumult of war, the clash of arms, the moans of the wounded and the death rattle.'[13]

Like the Psalmist, Rotgeber underscores his questions with deep faith:

'My spirit has acquired new strength, my faith in the God of Israel is even stronger. I firmly believe that Israel will not perish. Only my flesh, unfortunately, doesn't keep step with the spirit . . . I am not afraid, faith strengthens me. A week ago I had a talk with God (do you laugh! It is only with him that I am able to converse!). The thought came to me that our sufferings will end soon and punishment will overtake our inhuman persecutors.'[14]

Factual events in the ghetto give rise to appeals to God to intervene. For example, Rotgeber describes how, from his window, he watched people being hauled out into the street and marched to *Umschlagplatz*:

'A shiver of terror overwhelmed me, but I stayed where I was. I watched, I watched right to the end. A terrible pain overwhelmed me, my sick heart contracted but I, turning my eyes towards the heaven, looked for angels who would take these unhappy brothers of mine under their care. The sky was clear, there was no rumble of an approaching storm to herald God's wrath. The God of Israel has turned his gaze from us. He has forgotten about his poor children. The enemy lords it over us and there is no punishment for him . . . The rivers of blood flow (and are) swollen. Their terrible groans go before them. The aura illuminates everything. The sounds reach to the heavens – Where is your Kingdom, O God? Where is your reign over the world? . . . "A voice crying in the wilderness". No one hears – no one sees . . . Prayers and beseechings are in vain. Jehovah has turned his gaze from us. The God of Israel is very angry. How can we appease him? When will there be an end to our sufferings? Has God, *Shojresh beisrael*, abandoned us? And are we not necessary to you any more? Your houses of prayer are destroyed. The Divine sanctuary has been shamed and in the Warsaw bazaars they hammer the holy Pentateuch rolls into wooden walls for their market stalls. There is no vileness that has not been meted out to us. And you, God of Israel, you see this and you remain silent?'[15]

Questing and questioning, Karol Rotgeber tells his brother, 'Be of good cheer, although Israel has been given a bitter penance; yet the only power in the world which might destroy us is the power of God. We bear the punishment of our sins, but God in his mercy will turn aside the total disaster.'[16]

Many people voiced the thought that God seemed to be punishing his people. Calel Perechodnik reacted angrily to this suggestion: 'I couldn't listen when a normal, adult person, in addition a Jew, affirmed that the murder of the Jewish nation arose because of sins committed by the Jews against God, that all this cataclysm is God's will and was foretold by the Jewish prophets.'[17]

In Rotgeber's case his understanding of God's judgement forces him to turn to God in continuous intercession: 'Almighty God . . . Israel has suffered enough persecution. Jehovah, our God . . . remember our prophets . . . save your lost sheep . . . forgive us our sins . . . let yourself be placated.'[18]

Following the tradition of the Talmud, Rotgeber appeals to Rachel who weeps for her children and is not comforted 'because they are no more' (Jeremiah 31.15): 'Arise, beloved Mother Rachel! Look at your children now! Hurry to God while there is time. You suffered during your life. The God of Israel will listen to you. Hurry, hurry, O dearest Mother – time is already pressing. Otherwise the silence of the graveyard will reign and the seed of Israel will not exist . . .'[19]

But even within the 'silence of the graveyard' Rotgeber continues to hope:

'Everything is empty . . . phantoms, skeletons . . . a fearful clamour in heaven. Mount Sinai begins to smoke. Thunder and lightning strike. A powerful voice is heard throughout the world, "I am the Lord your God who brought you out of slavery in the land of Egypt" . . . O, my Israel, don't despair. You will rise from the dead, you and your holy faith. The time has already come! Your sins are wiped out. The bright sun lowers the hem (of its garment) towards you. Then tomorrow will be clear. The day of wonder will come . . . God will be the only victor. Only he will reign. The ravages of war, the murders, the satanic thoughts will come to nothing. The fusty fumes of Europe will blow away, no trace will remain. The arrogant, shameless murders will disappear. Peace on earth will arise to the glory of God . . . Do you hear this and see it, O

Jehovah? I have become a Titan, a giant, the smouldering lights of my eyes have caught fire, my arms have acquired strength and I raise them as Moses our saint once did, in order to tip the scales of victory in favour of Jehudah.'[20]

Rotgeber's diary ends as it began, with an expression of trust in God:

'But you, O God, know better what will be and what it is necessary to do. May your name be glorified for all ages! Long live Israel! Let the standard of Zion be raised on high! Warsaw 12 June 1943.'[21]

The rabbis of the ghetto had prepared a prayer in December 1942. Called 'prayer composed especially for the present moment', it was to be said on behalf of those who had been carried away in the mass murder of the summer. Psalms 94 and 42 were to be read before the prayer:

'Ruler of the Universe! Lord of the world! Hear our weeping and the groaning of our hearts, look at our sufferings and torments – and aid us in our great need. We, descendants of Abraham, Isaac and Jacob, are persecuted, destroyed and driven like sheep to the slaughter. Let your will be done, dear God, so that you might protect us from misfortune and put to naught the evil and cruelty of the enemy.'[22]

In the writings of the ghetto the phrase 'like sheep – or lambs – to the slaughter' was often used pejoratively. Here the rabbis give the words their deeper, biblical sense.

One of the rabbis who helped compose the prayer was Klonimus Kelmish Shapiro, from Piaseczno, outside Warsaw. In his homilies in the ghetto Rabbi Shapiro has to address the sufferings of his hearers as well as retaining the holy light of the Torah. At first he saw the Nazi persecution as another link in the long chain of Jewish suffering. In a sermon composed for the Feast of Hanukah, December 1941 he asks:

121

'Why is it that we are more moved by present sufferings than by all those sufferings which befell Israel in the past? Why is it that when we used to read in Scripture, the Talmud or Midrash about Israel's sufferings from the remotest times until our present day, our faith didn't weaken, but it is weak now? For those who say that Israel has never witnessed such sufferings as these are in error . . .'[23]

However, as the misery and suffering in the ghetto increased, Rabbi Shapiro found that words had failed him. On 28 February 1942, he said:

'We are still living through very bitter and unpleasant experiences . . . Even someone who used to strengthen himself and other Jews is now too exhausted to find inner strength; he is tired of seeking consolation. Even if he wanted to pull himself together and deliver a few remarks of comfort and encouragement, he would have no words to do so, because he has already said everything he could many times in the course of these continuing days of crisis. The words are hackneyed now, they produce no effect on him or his listeners.'[24]

The wellsprings have dried, says Rabbi Shapiro. The inspiration, joy and light of the Holy Scriptures seem to have nothing more to say. Rabbi Shapiro wrestles with this problem. He sums it up in a homily delivered on 14 March 1942:

'The time will come when we will be surprised at ourselves . . . Have I not been led to despair? Am I not constantly on the verge of tears – and sometimes indeed I do break down? How then am I to study Torah? How am I to find the strength for creative thinking about the Torah and Hasidism? There are times when a person tortures himself with the thought, "Can I find nothing in my heart but stupor, nothing that might make me pull myself together and study, in spite of personal cares and those which have fallen in such multiplicity upon Israel?"

And then the person says to himself, "Am I not driven to despair? I have so many reasons for weeping, my whole life is dark and gloomy... The House of Israel... has never experienced anything like this. May God have mercy on us and save us from their hands in the twinkling of an eye.'"[25]

In a sermon in January 1942 Rabbi Shapiro explored the theme of suffering as a sacrifice. He develops the thought expressed by a great Hebrew scholar, Rashi – that in the Temple in Jerusalem the dish of ashes on the altar became an instrument of praise. (In *Text in the Face of Extermination* Dr Leociak explains that the Hebrew name for this instrument, *magrefah*, literally means 'shovel'):

When the sacrifice was placed on the altar and (burnt) and turned into ashes, we could see the greatness of the sacrifice from the quantity of ash which remained... But see, this same tool which was used to gather up the sacrificial ashes gave out the loudest music. The entire music of the Temple was a remembrance of the sacrifice offered to God... and even the *magrefah* played its part in this too, so that great compassion was awakened in heaven and speedy salvation for Israel.'[26]

The esoteric word play of the rabbinical study became shockingly apposite in the murder of the Holocaust. The sacrificial lambs were literally to be burnt, as the letter about 'Uncle's wedding' had warned. But out of his pain and questioning Rabbi Shapiro discovered God even in his seeming absence. God is not silent because he has rejected his suffering people – he is silent because he suffers so much that he has withdrawn into the innermost chamber of the cosmos to weep there in hiding:

'God, blessed be he, may be found in his inner chamber, weeping, so that one who pushes himself in and comes close to him by means of studying Torah, weeps together with God, and studies Torah with him. This is what makes the difference: the weeping, the pain which someone bears in solitude may lead him to despair and break him, so that he becomes incapable of action. But when someone pours out his tears with God – then that weeping strengthens him. He weeps – and this weeping increases his strength; he is broken – but finds courage to study and teach.'[27]

During the Uprising, Rabbi Shapiro was transported to the work camp of Trawniki, along with Emanuel Ringelblum and other leaders of the Warsaw Jewish community. Here he found 15 rabbis who had taken an oath that nothing would separate them and none would seek his own means of escape. A way of escape opened up in August 1943, when Dr Ringelblum was smuggled out of the camp, but Rabbi Shapiro chose to die with his spiritual brothers.

The purpose of this book has been to tell the story of the Warsaw ghetto through the stories of people for whom the written word, even if it was simply scrawled on a cellar wall or scribbled on a postcard flung from a death train was a last act of bearing witness, the last evidence that they had existed at all. The amount of ash, said Rabbi Shapiro, indicates the greatness of the holocaust. It will never blow away – nor will the voices of those who journeyed 'into the unknown', into the realms of death, ever be silent. Let us leave them now. Their luggage is packed. The wagons are already on the tracks and Dyna is writing her last postcard:

'We're writing what we think will be our last card. We've all to leave on Wednesday at 5 a.m. Our modest luggage is in front of us, already packed and the wagons are already waiting for us at the station. Our spirits are terribly sad at the thought that we only have this one last night to sleep at home, and then tomorrow we set off on our wandering into the world. Who knows whither – nor where fate will take us, it's hard to imagine our life, what awaits us, what will be . . .'[28]

Notes

1 *Chronicle.*
2 *Survive.*
3 *Memoirs.*
4 Calel Perechodnik, *Am I a Murderer? (Czy jeslem mordercą),* ed. Pawet Szapiro, Shalom Foundation, Warsaw 1993.
5 *Am I a Murderer?*
6 *Am I a Murderer?*
7 *Am I a Murderer?*
8 *Am I a Murderer?*
9 *Memoirs.*
10 *Song of the Murdered Jewish Nation,* quoted in Irena Maciewska (ed.), *Martyrdom and Extermination (Męczeństwo i Zagłada Żydów),* Krajowe Agencje Wydawnicza, Warsaw 1988.
11 Quoted in *Text.*
12 *Text.*
13 *Text.*
14 *Text.*
15 *Text.*
16 *Text.*
17 *Am I a Murderer?*
18 *Text.*
19 *Text.*
20 *Text.*
21 *Text.*
22 *Text.*
23 *Text.*
24 *Text.*
25 *Text.*
26 *Text.*
27 *Text.*
28 *Letters.*

Poems from Ghetto
(Lion Publishing 1989)

As was mentioned in the Prologue, for many years Jewish issues were not discussed in Poland and the only obvious pointer in Warsaw in the 1960s to the Holocaust was the monument to the heroes of the ghetto. Much later on, in the 1980s, books such as Ringelblum's *Chronicle* and Grynberg's *Memoirs from the Warsaw Ghetto* began to appear in Polish bookshops. In 1988 I happened to be in Warsaw and came across both these books. When I realized that people had buried their diaries and memoirs under the ground I became absolutely convinced that in whatever small way I could, I must let those silenced voices be heard once again. So I worked on a complete book of poems which I called *Ghetto*. I've included some of these poems here.

Night

'Ich dank dir Gott, az ich bin a id'.
Later the cry will be: 'Ich dank az ich bin . . .'
when everyone else has ceased to be,
when nightfall brings more terrors than the day,
when hunger strikes as hard as the SS
and 'selection' becomes a pseudonym for death.
B'shona haba b'jerushalaim: Next year in Jerusalem.

Raisins and almonds

Lullaby. Hear the golden goat cry:
almonds for sale:
raisins and almonds fresh from the tree.
Hush now, don't wail . . .
Here are almonds for you and raisins for me.
Sleep, sleep, little child.
How still those bairns lie!
Dream raisins and almonds;
the golden goat's cry
ends where a bright ladder touches the sky.
Sleep, sleep, hush-a-bye.

The sun is smiling in the sky.
I'm ten years old, I will not die –
yet every day
transports take our friends away.
B'shona haba b'jerushalaim: Next year in Jerusalem.

Tightrope Walker

Let's all hold hands – it's safer so. Now try
to walk a tightrope stretched against the sky.
Don't lose your balance, please, don't fall, for no
nice safety net is waiting down below.
There's nothing left except this length of rope.
Hold your head high. It is our only hope.
The ghetto walls don't keep the death trains out –
and even those who guess that gas awaits
think silence is the kindest way to care,
keep starving homesick children from despair.
So Gabriella works with paints, engrossed,
forgets the feel of hunger, pain and loss.

Don't go to Uncle's Wedding

She is eleven now, and it is May.
Next week she's turned to ashes, blown away.

A wave of benediction

'We weep later in full sunlight, never at the precise moment'
(Oskar Milosz)

Light, a wave of benediction
washes the evening sky.
We are all implicated,
We, the ones who did not die,
the then unborn, who grew to learn
the meaning of the six-pointed star.
The fires have gone out
and we are cold.
Our tragedy – to have ignored;
our loss – that we refused to know,
even that medieval Jewry had been put to flight,
or that waves of later hatred brought them west
from Odessa and Lublin to sew shirts
in London, set up a stall in Leeds,
(nothing more than sixpence or less than a penny here!)
From Vilnius to Glasgow, from the Niemen to New York . . .
The flame, though bright, seemed foreign.
We did not stretch out our hands,
despised the rock from which was hewn
the knowledge of the Nameless,
hope of justice for the poor.
Who fasts now at Yom Kippur?

The Dead

We hold within ourselves shadowy beings,
of no relevance –

but survival depends
on remembering.
They gave us life.
We once slept, unseen, within.
Now – and this is their bequeathing –
we continue their uncharted path
long after memories fade,
more frail than ash.

Furnaces

Beside the furnace, yawning fire of hell,
the Venice Senate marks our 'Lebensraum':
where copper once was forged, now Jews must dwell.
In Aragon the Hebrews are controlled;
Ferrara, Frankfurt, ghettos become homes;
for Christendom deems Jews are doomed to hell.
On Eve of Av Pope Paul rings out his bell,
creates a street for Jews in Christian Rome:
on Tiber's bank two thousand Hebrews dwell.
In cramped surroundings, schools and theatres tell
that learning flourished lacking doge or dome
beside the furnace, yawning fire of hell
till liberty proclaims its world-wide call:
belief is free, ghettos are overthrown.
Where copper once was forged no Jew need dwell.
The Nurenberg decrees exclude, expel.
New ghettos rise, essential rights disowned.
Beside the furnace Jews are marked for hell;
where death is forged, despair and madness dwell.

O, angel of death, dark being of terror,
we huddle beneath your wings,

sleep happed[1] in rags, no food, no fire.
our unwashed bodies are pressed close
for warmth, yet these sticks of bones
can give no heat, hardly totter to our tomb.

Holy things are overthrown
The God of Abraham, Isaac, Jacob,
of burning bush or cloven stone,
has not come down to save us.
We prayed and died alone.

Synagogues topple in ruins,
ancient plate is melted down.
Pious lips force out shamed spittle;
beards are plucked out, sidelocks shorn.

Guards search in young men's trousers,
hoist a rabbi's robes.
We fast, we weep, O, Israel:
nothing can atone.

They build the walls
It is finished. It is the end of everything.
The play is ended, the masks are down,
and who is now the hero, who the clown?
Every nightmare, every fear,
every unleashed horror happens here,
behind these walls.
Now each uncensored, savage fairy tale,
each destructive demon is revealed
where exit is forbidden – sh'ma Israel –
and escape can be only into a desert,
into lion's jaws.

Poems from Ghetto

Protest is vain,
only the voices of starved children
cry out frustration, pain
into the unfriendly silence of the night.

Hunger grows within our walls.
Wild children howl, lie down and die.
We barter, thieve, beg, trade.
We want to live. We learn the rules,
take off our caps and school
our bodies to bend
low low low
before sticks and blows.
Our guards have the right to shoot on sight.
They shoot with cameras too,
metres of film, true, yet untrue.

Passover

Linen and bread and herbs are spread
while we weep for our beloved dead.
Our lintels are covered with blood.
O, Angel of death, pass over, pass by:
B'shona haba b'jerushalaim: Next year in Jerusalem.

But we work. Everyone wants to work. Work
is the only way for Jewish slaves to live.
We work in factories for German gain:
huge enterprises based in Berlin
need our sweat.
We work while executions multiply.
We work for fear that we too shall be shot,
our twitching bodies left to rot.

We work for fear that we too shall be sent
'further east' in sealed trucks.
The 'Jewish question' has been solved:
five thousand daily are packaged, shipped, dissolved.
Death is never more than a shouted word, a levelled
    arm away.

Rabbi Yechiel

Terror mounts. Artists, writers, rabbis meet to celebrate
(age old Jewish way which makes slaves great).
Hebrew, Yiddish words, banned, exalted, free
punctuate the horror pressing all around.
The very ground,
dumb earth, questions the sullen sky.
Wilno. Chełmno. A whole nation dies.
Blood of babies, desecration, official lies:
Familien nicht getrennt!
Rabbi Yechiel presides. His listeners note
polished shoes, his personal style, his speech.
'Hope against hope! Surely a limit must be reached?'
Protest is cleanliness, a well-cut coat.

The SS seek 'volunteers'.
'Workers for Smolensk'. A random round-up.
Rabbi Yechiel shows official papers:
'Sir, I am unfit for travel, being over fifty years . . .'
'Unfit for travel – means: fit to die!' The officer knows
the rules, shoots. 'Blut!'
Black boots stamp out the Rabbi's epitaph.
His crumpled corpse is trampled like a leaf.

Music in the ghetto – Maria Eisenstadt[2]

On Leszno Street a pre-war picture house
becomes a concert hall. The ghetto's full
of melodies which shine across each pool
of black despair. Beggars tout tunes to ease
their hunger. Songs, ballads disappear
as, promised bread, families volunteer
for journeys 'further east'; are first to hear
the gas. Can music sweeten nightmares, fear;
do more than rabbi, cantor, psalm or God?
'Ave Maria, young maid, full of grace . . .'
Defying censorship, a solo voice
soars clear and strong. Violins shiver, sob.
Her listeners weep, last accolade of tears.
A bullet ends her songs, her eighteen years.

No words

I stood on guard between broken attic boards,
saw a hand reach out, a head appear.
O, God, they're here!
But mother was too weak to hide. 'Go,
save yourselves,' she said.

No words. Guilt, horror, hatred, fear
and yet the need to live is strong,
get documents, listen to official lies.
I went to work. Next day they closed the gates.
We heard pistol shots, hellish hue and cry
and scattered like field mice
scampering to each threatened sheaf
while sickles slice the harvest.

Don't go to Uncle's Wedding

My family's nest
has been ransacked by well–armed rats.
'Daddy, do your best
to find us. We're lost,
Mummy and I, scheduled for the train,
but maybe fate will be kind
and we'll all meet again.'

No words, no words to describe my pain.

Umschlagplatz

This is the place. Selection has been made.
People are sorted, anguished and afraid.
We sold our clothing, wedding rings, procured
what food we could. All we have now is stored
in rucksacks. Ignorant of their design:
exterminate, make Warschau *Judenrein*,
we stand in July heat, September rain,
like patient cattle board each waiting train.
We have no choice. They beat and shoot. Our route,
defined by death, is mapped. Our minds are numb
with fear, bereavement, hunger. We still long
to build another life, sing woeful songs
for those we dared not mourn. New horrors come.
The engine jolts. We travel to our fate.

Janusz Korczak, two poems

A marvellous summer moon
illumines hopeless streets.
I shall be vapour soon.
Death harvests all we are,
earth, water, air.

Poems from Ghetto

To be born, to live – we learn;
may we not learn to die?
And, after death, what then?
Every step we take is fraught
with death.
Each dying child I touch
teaches me death needs time and thought.
But last night in my prayer,
though I felt well-being stir,
I could not bless this world at war.
I sat quietly, breathing deep,
feeling muscles, mind relax
amidst children in untroubled sleep,
yet the blessing would not come.
My upraised hands grew slack.
I was powerless and dumb.
Without blessing, healing will not come.

No birds fly in the ghetto,
No flower grows.
Pavements are crowded, hunted,
blood daily flows.

Those who weep among new graves
find comfort in old prayers.
Children's voices, the worn black book –
these reassure.

Closely wrapped in folds of prayer
the man stands so still
that sparrows flutter to his hands,
settle on his shawl.

Don't go to Uncle's Wedding

Birds and children trust their saint
who begs their food,
sits beside dying beggar children,
protects his brood.

Protects, but cannot save them,
in the August raid.
Singing, travels with the children,
'We shall sleep, don't be afraid.'

The plan's conceived from start to end in hell

Throughout the summer people are marched here —
some fifteen thousand is the daily score.
They bring their luggage, but so vast the crowd
a bare six kilos only is allowed,
so people throw clothes, towels, soap away;
still hope they'll work, buy, sell, not die.
Some needs must still be met. There is no place.
The butcher guards crack whips, kill at will, curse,
stamp useless passports, mock, make torment worse.
Trucks come, and people push on board. The sides
are sealed. Sentries guard the roof with guns.
The route is secret. Drivers dare not tell.
The plan's conceived from start to end in hell.

After the selection

After the selection the ghetto shrinks inside.
The only children left are 'criminals' we hide,
who have no right to breathe or make a noise.
Each new blockade contorts their faces, eyes.

Poems from Ghetto

There are few women; no one to cook or clean.
How did they do it? we wonder, wishing we had seen
the marvel that mothers laundered without soap,
and without provisions served us soup.

We have no family lives, we are truly slaves.
Our children were snatched from us, they stole our wives.
Only work is left for us, without food or pay,
yet without this work we're all earmarked to die.

Rumour is our daily food. It wasn't true,
they say, about Treblinka, in spite
of that legendary 'one that got away'
with news of naked corpses, wagon-loads of clothes.
'Our families really have gone "further east",' they say,
'So and so got a postcard, stamped, and everyone is well,
they work, they have enough to eat . . .'

Another rumour spreads: the children have returned:
two thousand pale children have appeared.

Ah, little lost ones, beloved ghosts,
you have come back here to haunt us, who have lost hope.
I think that when the tale of our tragedy is fully told
grieving parents will hold out waiting arms
to welcome long lost children, white as Russian snow,
fair and strong as birches, hair shining in the sun –
then turn away in sorrow, deluded by a dream.

For our children are dust and ashes
who dance in every sunbeam,
fade away in rain,
sting our eyes like snowflakes,
soft and sharp as tears.
This is the truth we chronicle:
our heritage, our heir.

Resistance

In death the bitter truth is, life goes on.
We leave a silent, curtained room
and step into the traffic's roar,
order flowers, food,
turn from grave or urn
to find children playing, snow, sun.

Each small normality
strikes like a blow between the eyes –
at least in normal times.

Here, every day is squalid, mean,
an unvoiced scream.
We make forays into plundered homes
for food no one now owns.

Our route lies underground
through holes cut in adjoining walls
throughout the beleaguered town.
The death penalty awaits
any who go through the ghetto gates,
where plotters debate:
should the ghetto have arms?

Poems from Ghetto

A single Nazi death means: exterminate.
But young people meet secretly, talk till late . . .

Brothers, fight!

Young people read graffiti scrawled
by now dead fingers on hidden walls:
brothers, fight!
Gaunt nuns
come to the ghetto walls
with bread and guns.
Starving boys and girls with hand-grenades
resist machine gun fire. The Germans flee!
Tanks roll in – do not return,
but the ghetto starts to burn.
Choked with smoke, shot down, resisters fight fires.
The hunters smoke out human prey
who go to ground – in cellars, sewers –
Cellars where fighters hide are filled with gas,
sewers blown up with dynamite.
Whole streets are razed.
A city burns to smoke out slaves!
The world is dumb.
Gunshot still comes in sporadic bursts,
a whiff of warm air is a sign
of human hidden life,
a sign for the hunters to ignite
their charges, set off dynamite.
A sign to us to carry on the fight,
though death is closing round us thick as night.
No one will dig our graves. These poisonous dens
shall hold for ever our unshrouded bones.

Elegy

Death struck them day and night,
carried them beyond our sight,
from ransacked houses, fearful streets,
gunfire, blows, booted feet:
musicians, traders, young and old,
scholars, craftsmen, girls with child.
Their lullabies, their stories, dreams
are turned to rubble which rebuilds homes,
shroud dwelling-blocks like autumn mist.
Passers-by may glimpse a fleeting ghost,
or hear a whispered word: remember us.

Written in Warsaw and Edinburgh, 1988. The collection fin-
ishes here – 'remember us'. But the story goes on:

Dr Marek Edelman lays flowers on the monument,
19th April, 1999

He brings flowers to the monument,
walking with firm steps despite the cold
and unremitting weight
of five decades:
Walking freely now where then flames flowered
and pavements melted beneath his fighting feet.
Fuelled by gas, ceremonial fires
honour his young comrades
who – with this one survivor – plotted a fight
they knew they could not win.
Slowly he mounts steep steps, a grassy mound
where they died at their own hands –
lovers, sweethearts, mothers, sons.
Rubble covers their bones . . .

He halts, moves on.
A slow procession follows in the biting wind.
And when the last person has gone
the April dusk
pours down snowflakes thick as memories;
buries formal roses, wired lilies.
Brief candle flames which children lit go out.
Across windows which overlook the memorial route
unresisting curtains, drawn against the dark,
exclude the elemental ghosts which haunt the night.

Notes

1 Scots for wrapped.
2 Maria Eisenstadt is the Marysia Ajzensztadt, the nightingale of
   the ghetto mentioned in Chapter 3.

Further Reading

History:
Davies, Norman, *God's Playground*, Columbia University Press, New York, 1982. A best-selling history of Poland which includes chapters on the Holocaust and the situation of Jews in Poland after 1945.
Dawidowicz, Lucy S., *The War against the Jews 1933–45*, Holt, Rinehart and Winston, 1975. Covers the growing pressure on the Jews of Europe and gives the story of Polish Jewry in general, but includes useful material on the Warsaw ghetto.
Dobson, R. B., *The Jews of Medieval York and the Massacre of March 1190*, University of York Borthwick Paper No. 45, 1989. A salutary reminder of an English episode in the story of ethnic cleansing.
Gutman, Yisrael, *The Jews of Warsaw, 1939–43*, Midland Books, Indiana University Press, 1989. Professor Gutman was a young participant in the Ghetto Uprising. This is a definitive history of Warsaw's Jewish Community from the outbreak of the Second World War.
Gilbert, Martin, *The Holocaust*, Fontana, 1986. Covers the Holocaust in detail.

Personal stories:
Bauman, Janina, *Winter in the Morning*, Virago, 1986. Describes a young person's experiences in the ghetto and in hiding.
Karski, Jan, *The Story of a Secret State*, Miflim Hodder, 1944.
Lewin, Abraham, *A Cup of Tears*, Blackwell, 1988. A member of Oneg Shabat whose ghetto diary terminates abruptly on the eve of January 1943.
A Polish Doctor, *I saw Poland Suffer*, Lindsay Drummond, London,

Further Reading

1941. A little book by an anonymous author which gives an eyewitness account as the Nazi noose was being drawn around Poland.

Wiesel, Elie, *Night*, Penguin Books, 1981. Nobel prizewinner Elie Wiesel's powerful and unforgettable account of Auschwitz.

Zylberberg, Michael, *A Warsaw Ghetto Diary 1939–45*, Vallentine Mitchell, London, 1969. An account of a survivor.

Biography:

Lifton, Betty Jean, *The King of Children*, Chatto and Windus, 1988. The story of Dr Janusz Korczak and his children.

Wood, Thomas E., *Karski, How One Man Tried to Stop the Holocaust*, John Wiley & Sons, New York, 1994. The story of the Polish courier who took first-hand accounts of Nazi atrocities in the Warsaw ghetto and the extermination camps out to the Allies in 1942.

Fiction:

Hersey, John, *The Wall*, Cardinal Giant edition, Pocket Books, Inc., USA, 1954. A novel set in the Warsaw ghetto. Although the characters are imaginary and have a life of their own, readers of this book will find them familiar.

Schwarz-Bart, Andre, *The Last of the Just*, MJF Books, Fine Communications, New York, © 1960 by Atheneum House, Inc. A prize-winning novel which covers the story of the Levy family from medieval York to Auschwitz, including Poland and Nazi Germany.

Other:

Polen, Nehemia, *The Holy Fire: The Teachings of Rabbi Kalonymus Shapiro, the Rabbi of the Warsaw Ghetto*, Jason Aronson Inc., Northvale, New Jersey, 1994, 1999.

Snell, Adrian, with Jenny Robertson, *Children of Exile*, Word Books, 1991. A Christian musician's exploration of the Holocaust, with a Foreword by Rabbi Hugo Gryn.

Children's Drawings and Poems, Terezin 1942–44, Statni Zidovske Museum, Prague, 1959. An album of work by children in a Czech ghetto.